Six new AMERICAN HERITAGE JUNIOR LIBRARY *books are
published each year. Titles currently available are:*

COVER: *This nineteenth-century painting by George H. Boughton called,* Pilgrims Going to Church, *shows the citizens of Plymouth walking to one of their Sabbath services. They met from eight to twelve o'clock in the morning, and then met again in the afternoon.*

TITLE PAGE: *The eighteenth-century artist who painted this picture of the landing of the Pilgrims at Plymouth in December, 1620, made two errors: he depicted the* Mayflower *as a ship of his own time, and he imagined that the Pilgrims were greeted by Indians.*

CONTENTS PAGE: *John Bunyan, shown here asleep, was the most popular Puritan author in England after his famous book* Pilgrim's Progress *appeared in 1678. It tells of the pilgrimage of its hero, Christian, toward the Celestial City. Because the Puritans were eager to learn how to walk the path to salvation, the book was reprinted many times.*

FRONT END SHEET: *Painted by Pieter Bruegel the Younger, this version of the 1566 work* The Massacre of the Innocents *by Pieter Bruegel the Elder was based on the Biblical story of King Herod's massacre of the male children of Judea. Both painters had seen Catholic Spain's brutal military occupation of the rebellious Low Countries. Conditions grew worse in 1567, especially for Protestants, when the Duke of Alba became commander of the Spanish forces and set up the courts of the Inquisition in Belgium and Holland.*

BACK END SHEET: *Courts of the Inquisition, like this one in Spain—so greatly feared by the Pilgrims and their Dutch hosts—were still in operation in the early nineteenth century when this picture was painted by Francisco Goya, the Spanish artist. A witchcraft trial is in progress; the accused witches are wearing pointed caps and robes. Heretics seized by the Inquisition could be fined, imprisoned, tortured, or even burned at the stake.*

OPPOSITE: *This 1670 woodcut of Richard Mather, the scholarly minister who developed the Puritan system of church government in Massachusetts, was the first woodcut made in New England. Mather was also a translator of the Psalms included in the Puritans'* The Whole Book of Psalmes (1640), *which came to be better known as the* Bay Psalm Book.

THE PILGRIMS AND PLYMOUTH COLONY

HURON LIBRARY MEDIA CENTERS

ILLUSTRATED WITH PAINTINGS, PRINTS, DRAWINGS, AND MAPS OF THE PERIOD

THE PILGRIMS

AND PLYMOUTH COLONY

BY THE EDITORS OF

AMERICAN HERITAGE
The Magazine of History

NARRATIVE BY

FEENIE ZINER

IN CONSULTATION WITH

GEORGE F. WILLISON
AUTHOR OF *Saints and Strangers*

PUBLISHED BY

AMERICAN HERITAGE
PUBLISHING CO., INC.
NEW YORK

Foreword

Who were the Pilgrims? What kind of people were they? What did they stand for? What adventurous travels through a sea of troubles led them across the Atlantic to establish at Plymouth in 1620 the first permament English settlement in New England? Once "planted" on our shores, what did they do? Why is the Pilgrim story so essential a part of our American heritage?

Answers to these and other questions appear in this book which highlights in authentic form and graphic detail the major events in the lives of the Pilgrim Fathers and their families. Not once, but many times, the Pilgrims launched themselves upon the most dangerous of adventures, and no matter what the odds against them, nothing could stop them or divert them from their course.

Theirs is a story of great courage and deep conviction. In an age of royal tyranny, they stood steadfast in their belief and desire that there should be a more democratic order of things. They stood ready to sacrifice their lives—as many of them did—to carry out their ideals.

Among other things, the Pilgrims demanded the right to "freedom of conscience," which is one aspect of the still larger right to freedom of thought and speech. The Pilgrims were saying that they wished to worship as they pleased, and intended to do so.

This was a very dangerous position to take at a time when English law required everyone to attend Church of England services—and no other. Steady refusal to attend such services could bring a heavy fine, or hanging, or even burning at the stake. But the Pilgrims were not dismayed and went on holding their secret and highly illegal religious meetings at the risk of life and limb.

Harried by church and state authorities, the Pilgrims escaped from England and took refuge in Holland, where they lived as exiles for some dozen years—first in Amsterdam, later in Leyden. They were fairly happy there, for Holland had granted religious toleration for all sects, being the only country in Europe at the time to be so enlightened.

It was their growing poverty that decided the Pilgrims to seek their fortunes in the New World. Like the many many millions who in time followed them across the Atlantic, the Pilgrims were seeking a chance to better their worldly lot. Let it never be forgotten that our country was founded and largely built by "foreigners" of many different nationalities, religions, and ways of life.

In September, 1620, the *Mayflower* set sail on her historic voyage, having on board about forty Pilgrims ("Saints") from Leyden and even more "Strangers" recruited by the London Merchant Adventurers financing the enterprise.

What happened on the voyage and after the landing at Plymouth is well told in this book: the threatened mutiny on the *Mayflower*; the signing of the Mayflower Compact, one of the great democratic documents in American history; the General Sickness during which half the *Mayflower* company died within three or four months; the very helpful friendships made with such Indians as Samoset, Squanto, and Massasoit; the struggle to grow or find enough to eat in the early years; the first American Thanksgiving; the clash with Thomas Morton of Merry Mount; and other main adventures in the Pilgrims' always eventful lives.

This, above all, should be remembered about the Pilgrims: though they suffered greatly for their beliefs, they came through to triumph because they had the courage of their convictions. Such courage is priceless—and few people have possessed it in any age, including our own.

GEORGE F. WILLISON

FIRST EDITION

LIBRARY OF CONGRESS CATALOGUE CARD NUMBER: 61-14735

Contents

JOHN WICKLIFFE

THE REFORMATION

The Pilgrims were rebels born in an age of turmoil. When they set sail on the *Mayflower* in 1620, bound for the New World, they left behind them an Old World which had been torn by religious wars and revolutions for more than a century, and an England which would struggle for full civil and religious freedom for another two centuries. The strong faith they brought with them to America had its roots in those long years of struggle known as the Reformation.

Ever since the countries of western Europe had adopted Christianity, they had been served by one church alone—the Roman Catholic Church. The Pope, as head of the Church, appointed all bishops. The power of the Pope was often greater than that of kings and emperors. Over the slow centuries of the Middle Ages the Church grew in riches until it owned one-third of all the property in Europe. Most of the common people labored (like the serf shown plowing the fields at left) on lands belonging to the lord of the castle. Few

These sketches of John Calvin (above) were made around 1563 by one of the students at his Geneva academy. Lucas Cranach painted this portrait (left) of his close friend Martin Luther in 1534.

lords and fewer serfs could read. No serf could leave the land and take up a trade in town without his lord's permission. No serf had any voice in choosing his priest, his bishop, his lord, or his king. All were taught to believe that Pope, king, lord, and bishop had been set over them by the will of God.

One of the first and most important men to demand religious reform was the English scholar priest, John Wyclif (1328-1384). He spoke out against the iron authority of the Church. Wyclif believed that the Church had grown too wealthy, and that men were bound to obey neither priests nor bishops. He and his black-robed followers taught, instead, that all men had the right to read the Bible and to decide for themselves the way they wished to worship God. For this reason, he and two other scholars made the first complete English translation of the Vulgate (as the Latin Bible, then used by all Catholic Churches in Europe, is known).

Wyclif was persecuted in England, but his ideas lived on. A century after his death, Martin Luther (1483-1546) was born in Germany. In Wyclif's footsteps, he taught that men had no need of priests or bishops in obtaining God's grace. Like Wyclif, too, he translated the Bible—into his native German—and urged men to follow only its teachings. When a number of German princes who supported Luther were ordered to return to the Catholic Church in 1529, they *protested* against the ruling, and the word "Protestant"

was born. When Luther wrote that a "common *reformation* should be undertaken," he gave the Protestant Reformation its name. As early as 1536 there was no church but the Lutheran Church in Norway, Denmark, and Sweden. Luther also gained many supporters in northern and central Germany, but at the price of terrible wars which would continue between Lutherans and Catholics until 1648.

The religious reforms of the Frenchman John Calvin (1509-1564) were as important as those of Luther. Calvin left Catholic France, and in 1536 he went to Geneva, Switzerland, which had recently become a Protestant city. From there he spread his revolutionary ideas — including the belief that it was more important to obey the laws of the Bible than to obey the laws of Popes and bishops and kings. Calvin also taught his followers to be hardworking, sober, and thrifty, and to name their children after the men and women of the Old Testament. He sternly forbade them to go to plays, to play cards or to gamble, to read Catholic books, or to wear lace and jewels. Calvinists soon set up Reformed Churches in parts of Germany and Switzerland. The Scottish religious reformer John Knox came to Geneva in 1554 to study under Calvin. Six years later, after a year of civil war, Knox's Presbyterian Church had driven the Catholic Church from Scotland.

Reformed churches sprang up in Holland, then ruled by the devout Catholic Philip II of Spain. Some of Calvin's followers began

King Edward VI
(reigned 1547-53)

King Henry VIII
(reigned 1509-47)

Queen Mary I
(reigned 1553-58)

Queen Elizabeth I
(reigned 1558-1603)

looting Catholic property in the Netherlands, smashing window and statues in Catholic cathedrals. To stamp out Calvinism and t suppress rebellion, Philip sent an army to the Low Countries in 156 (see front end sheet). Many towns were besieged, and 18,000 Pro estant Dutch were executed by the Spanish. Fighting continued a various periods during the next eighty years, until Holland finall won complete freedom as a Protestant nation, in 1648.

The Huguenots (as the French Calvinists were known) set up Reformed Church in France in 1559. Eight civil wars—the Wars c Religion—were fought between Catholics and Huguenots in France In 1598, when peace came—for a time—King Henry IV grante Huguenots partial religious freedom.

In England, the history of the first hundred years of the Reforma tion was not as bloody as it had been in Holland, France, and Ge many. King Henry VIII's decision to break with the Catholic Churc and to make himself supreme head of the Protestant Church of Eng land, in 1534, was largely political. Once he had done so, he sol off the great landholdings which had belonged to the Catholic mor asteries, and placed English Bibles in all the churches in the land In order to study the Bible for themselves, many people began learr ing to read. Later, when Henry's Protestant son, Edward VI, came t the throne, the ideas of Luther and Calvin began to take stronge hold in England. After Edward died, his half sister Mary becam queen and forced England to return to Catholicism. Because he five-year rule saw 300 Protestant martyrs burned at the stake, she wa called "Bloody Mary." When her half sister, Elizabeth, began he forty-five year reign in 1558, England returned to Protestantism.

So it is in the age of Elizabeth that the Pilgrim story begins. Fo it was while she ruled as queen (1558-1603) that many of those wh later boarded the *Mayflower* began to live their lives.

The Pilgrims hated the elaborate ritual of Church of England services like this one, held at St. Paul's Cathedral, London, around 1618. King James I, who succeeded Queen Elizabeth upon the throne, is seated in the elevated box (rear), flanked by his family.

The month of April in the poet Edmund Spenser's Shepheardes Calender *was illustrated in 1611 with this picture of ladies playing lutes, flutes, harps, and viols. The lady at center may be Queen Elizabeth.*

Merrie England

William Brewster, organizer of the Pilgrim Church and its ruling elder in Plymouth, Massachusetts, was born in 1566 or 1567, in the early years of Queen Elizabeth's reign. The Queen was then a spinster of thirty-three, and William Shakespeare—the greatest poet of her splendid age—was only two years old.

No picture of William Brewster has been discovered, nor is there any record of his birthplace. His father, William, and his mother, Prudence, were well-to-do but not prominent people. In 1575 the Brewsters took their nine-year-old son to the "meane townlet" of Scrooby, Nottinghamshire, about one hundred and fifty miles north of London on the Great North Road.

There William Brewster senior began work as bailiff and receiver of Scrooby manor—a large landholding belonging to the Archbishop of York. Brewster collected rents from the hundreds of farms and villages on the manor. In return, he received just over three pounds per year, plus the right to use the buildings and grounds of the manor house itself. In 1576, Edwin Sandys became Archbishop of York and continued Brewster in his post. He and his sons, Edwin and Samuel, were to help the Brewsters on a number of occasions in the future. After 1588, Brewster also earned thirty pounds a year (a very good salary, in that century) for his additional job as postmaster.

Young William learned to read and write, and even studied Latin during the next five years. This was remarkable in itself, for in the England of Brewster's day, not one child in ten received schooling of any kind. In December, 1580, at the age of fourteen, William Brewster set off for Cambridge University. Cambridge and Oxford then functioned only as training schools for ministers of the Church of England. By order of Queen Elizabeth, that Church was Protestant. But for many years, radical churchmen—stirred by what they read in their Bibles or influenced from abroad by the ideas of Luther and Calvin—had been arguing that the Church was not Protestant enough.

Forty years earlier in 1539, when Elizabeth's father King Henry VIII had ruled that every church must set forth copies of the English Bible (not only on the altar, but also in the back of the church, for the common people to read) he never imagined how much struggle and bloodshed those Bibles would cause. A Church of England historian writes that when six copies were set up in St. Paul's in London, "people crowded eagerly into the cathedral all day long to listen to any who could and would read with an audible voice."

One of Henry's noblemen, the Duke of Norfolk, disliked this remarkable new interest in the Bible, saying, "I never read the Scriptures, nor never will read it. It was merry in England afore the new learning came up: yea, I would all things were as hath been in time past." King Henry himself grew displeased with the religious disputes that began to arise. He regretted that that "most precious jewel the word of God" was "disputed, rhymed, sung and jangled in every alehouse and tavern." He had not wanted the people to read the Bible too diligently. When Henry had made himself head of the Church of England, he had changed few of the Catholic forms of worship, for he hoped Englishmen would continue to attend services in the Church of England just as they had attended Mass when the Church was Catholic.

Henry forced all his subjects to attend his Church and conform to its beliefs. He did not want English Protestants to begin wrangling among themselves—as the Protestants in Europe were beginning to do. He was fearful of the power of Catholic Spain, and needed a unified England standing squarely behind him.

Many years later, when Elizabeth became queen, she did much as her father had done. She too forced all her subjects to attend church. Those who refused were sent to jail, without bail, until they promised to mend their ways. No books could be printed with-

out her permission. Her bishops had the power to question, imprison, hang, or burn at the stake anyone holding dangerous religious views. And many religious radicals in Elizabeth's day held dangerous views indeed.

Even the mildest critics felt that the Church of England did not practice the Christian faith as simply as it should. In reading their Bibles, they discovered no mention of many of the rituals they saw performed in church on Sunday. In 1578, Dr. Laurence Chaderton (who later helped translate the King James Version of the Bible) spoke of the Church and its traditions as a "huge masse of old and stinkinge workes." Because he and similar critics followed the word of the Bible so closely, bishops of the Church mocked them as "precise men." But the "precise men" would not be silenced. They spoke of the Church as a "pache of popery and a puddle of corruption," and warned that Christianity must be restored to its "ancient purity." From such words as these, those who hoped to reform the Church from within were sneered at, and called Puritans.

Other reformers held ideas that were still more radical and dangerous. Two years before William Brewster began studying at Cambridge, Robert Browne had preached such violent sermons there that he was forced to leave the university. He taught his followers (later called Brownists, or Separatists) that all worthy men, "were they ever so few," should *separate* from the Church of England and form congregations in which to worship as they chose. He told them that St. Paul himself had said, "Come out from among them, and be ye separate, saith the Lord, and touch not the unclean thing."

"Troublechurch" Browne, as he was

POR... QUI TOTO ORBE CELEBERRIMU...

This 1611 view of London (above) shows the city much as it must have appeared to the young William Brewster when he was in the employ of Sir William Davison. In the picture below, Queen Elizabeth I's gorgeously dressed courtiers are shown carrying their unmarried ruler to the wedding of Anne Russell, one of the Queen's maids of honor. The scene was painted by Marcus Gheeraerts the Younger in 1600.

known, was sent to jail soon after. Upon his release, he and his followers fled to Protestant Holland, where freedom of worship was permitted.

Since the Cambridge of the 1580's remained a strong center of Puritan thought, William Brewster must have listened to many sermons there which were almost as rousing as those of "Troublechurch" Browne. For it was at Cambridge that he was "first seasoned with ye seeds of grace and vertue." And it was there that he began to believe that Christianity should be returned to its "primative order, libertie & bewtie," and to think seriously of becoming a Separatist himself.

In Cambridge, too, Brewster may have known Christopher Marlowe (who was later to write two famous plays, *Tamburlaine the Great* and *Dr. Faustus*) for Marlowe was just two years ahead of him in school. It is almost certain that he knew John Penry (who was hanged thirteen years later, for printing pamphlets which attacked the Church) for he and Penry enrolled in the same college on the

This seventeenth-century print shows Cambridge University's beautiful spires and steepled towers. In Brewster's day, Cambridge—fed by the ideas of Renaissance and Reformation—was a seedbed of Puritan thought.

same day. Perhaps he also met Penry's friend John Greenwood, a Separatist hanged for his beliefs in 1593.

Nothing certain is known of the friends he made, but it is recorded that during his two years at college he gained "knowledge of ye Latine tongue & some insight in ye Greeke."

Brewster did not finish his studies at Cambridge. In 1582—probably through the good will of Archbishop Sandys—sixteen-year-old Brewster went to London to begin work as valet and confidential messenger for one of Queen Elizabeth's trusted diplomats, Sir William Davison. Since Davison was a Puritan, he was drawn to Brewster's "wisdom and godliness." He treated the boy more like "a sonne than a servante" and soon "trusted him above all others that were aboute him."

In this position, young Brewster may have glimpsed such brilliant figures at the Court of Queen Elizabeth as Sir Walter Raleigh; Sir Francis Drake; Robert Devereux, Earl of Essex; and Robert Dudley, Earl of Leicester.

In 1585, to give aid to the Dutch Protestants, Elizabeth sent an army of 6,000 men under Leicester to the Low Countries, then struggling to win their independence from Spain. When matters concerning an English loan to the

Dutch took Sir William Davison to Holland that same year, William Brewster traveled with him. They returned to England in 1586, when Davison's mission was completed.

Brewster might never have left the exciting life he led in Davison's service had it not been for the beautiful Mary, Queen of Scots. Mary was a Catholic, a cousin of Queen Elizabeth, and heir to the throne of England. After many unhappy events in Scotland, she had given up her throne to her son, James. When she fled to England, in 1568, Elizabeth put her in prison. Elizabeth suspected that Mary was urging Catholic Spain to invade England, so Mary could become queen. When an attempt was made to assassinate Elizabeth in 1586, men whispered that Mary was behind it. Rightly or wrongly, Elizabeth believed them.

Mary was tried and judged guilty in October of that year. Elizabeth signed Mary's death warrant and gave it to Sir William Davison, telling him to guard it carefully and not to use it without her express permission. When Davison later allowed the warrant to be put into effect, Mary was beheaded on February 8, 1587.

Elizabeth had wanted Mary killed, but she had no wish to be held respon-

Sir William Davison

sible for the execution. So, saying that Davison had not followed her orders to the letter, Elizabeth sent him to prison in the Tower of London. Though Davison was now in disgrace, for a year or more William Brewster continued to serve him.

That year—1588—was a year of turmoil in England. For when King Philip of Spain had learned of Mary's death, he sent his great fleet—the Spanish Armada—to attack the Protestant English and Dutch and to invade England. With the rest of his countrymen, Brewster must have rejoiced when Sir Francis Drake's ships won their great victory over the Spanish in the English Channel.

The following year, in 1589, Brewster learned that his father was ill. He was needed at home. Leaving the great world of Queen Elizabeth and William Shakespeare behind him forever, William Brewster turned his back on the busy city of London and started up the Great North Road for the tiny village of Scrooby.

Joris Hoefnagel's joyous picture (Wedding Feast at Bermondsey), painted in 159
shows the Merrie England of Queen Elizabeth at its best. The bridal processi

s seen here arriving at the feast, probably at the manor house of Sir Thomas
Pope. The building in the background, across the Thames, is the Tower of London.

The Scrooby Separatists

Upon William Brewster's return to Scrooby he found that his father had grown too feeble to attend to his many duties. So the son took over his father's work, collecting rents from the farms of the manor and managing the post house. Archbishop Sandys had died the year before, leaving his lands at Scrooby manor to one of his sons, Sir Samuel Sandys. A year after Brewster's return, in 1590, his own father died, and Sir Samuel asked William—now twenty-four years old—to continue permanently in the positions that Brewster senior had held. Young Brewster accepted.

By this date, Brewster must also have known Sir Samuel's brother, Edwin, who was to be of help to the Pilgrims more than thirty years later, when they were making their arrangements to come to America.

Toward the end of 1591 or early in 1592 William Brewster was married to Mary. Almost nothing is known of his wife except that her last name may have been Wentworth and that she was several years younger than he. Mary was later to sail on the *Mayflower* with her husband and two of their sons and spend the rest of her life in the New World. But at the time of their marriage, the Brewsters could never have imagined that so great an adventure lay ahead of them.

As postmaster of the little country town of Scrooby, it was part of Brewster's job to be always on the alert for travelers or royal couriers (mail carriers) passing up and down the Great North Road. He was required by law to keep three "good and sufficient" horses, together with saddles, bridles, and post bags for the use of the post riders, who carried only royal and official mail. He was also expected to keep an inn or tavern for the riders, as well as stables for their horses. So Brewster set aside the largest room in Scrooby manor, to serve as the tavern. He also supervised a bake house and a brew house where bread and beer were made for use in the tavern.

Far from the excitement of London life, Brewster kept in touch with the world by talking with travelers passing through Scrooby. In 1593, Mary bore him a son, Jonathan, and later a daughter, named Patience. Life was secure, peaceful, uneventful.

Or at least it felt that way in Scrooby. Elsewhere the battle between the bishops and their opponents went on. Separatists and Puritans continued their violent protests. They so much disliked the embroidered vestments of

The autocratic King James I (right), wearing full state regalia, was not to improve the lot of Separatists like William Brewster when he came to the throne of England in 1603.

The lives of the Brewsters and most of the other families in the countryside around Scrooby were centered on the land. The tilling of the soil in the spring and the harvesting of the crops in the fall were the most important events in their year. Their rural life made them feel akin to the ancient Hebrews, about whom they read in their Bibles. The woodcut above, made in 1569, shows English farmers doing their spring plowing with a team of oxen. The 1577 woodcut below shows a group of busy harvesters gathering up sheaves of grain in the fall.

the bishops that they spoke of them as the "rags of Rome." They despised the Church of England. "Bishops," they said, "were not lords over God's creation, as if the Church could not *be* without them."

Suddenly, short tracts (or pamphlets) ridiculing the bishops began flooding England. People read them and passed them from hand to hand. Written by one who signed himself "Martin Mar-Prelate," they were printed and circulated in secrecy. The name of the person who wrote them is still not known for certain. But in 1593 —the same year that Brewster's son Jonathan was born—the bishops had a man arrested, accused, and sent to trial for having operated the press where the tracts were printed. He was Brewster's old classmate at Cambridge, John Penry. That same year, Penry was hanged in London. For his writings against the Church, Penry's friend John Greenwood had also been hanged a few months earlier.

When Brewster heard the news of their tragic fate he must have thought of the fiery sermons against the Church he had once heard at Cambridge. He must also have shivered to think of the terrible power that the Queen and her bishops held over him and his fellow believers.

Perhaps Brewster spoke of the deaths of Penry and Greenwood with Richard Clyfton. Clyfton was rector (or minister) of the church of Babworth, not far from Scrooby, where William and Mary Brewster worshiped. Although a minister of the Church of England, Clyfton believed that the Church needed to be reformed. His Puritan turn of mind was so strong that people called him a "forward" preacher, as growing numbers of radical churchmen were then known.

Clyfton, who had a "great white beard," had studied at Cambridge and had been the "grave & reverend" rector at Babworth since 1586. Each Sunday the Brewsters—together with their children Jonathan and Patience— walked six miles across the Nottinghamshire countryside to hear Clyfton's "forward" Puritan sermons.

Many humble folk in the Scrooby district were converted to Clyfton's dangerous religious views. By 1602 there were several other churches in the nearby countryside which had begun to take on a Puritan character. One congregation of about 100 people met at Worksop, near Babworth. Another more radical group was to be found at Gainsborough, eight miles east of Scrooby.

One Sabbath day in 1602, at Clyfton's church in Babworth, Brewster met a twelve-year-old boy named William Bradford. He was the son of William and Alice Bradford, and he had been born in the nearby Yorkshire village of Austerfield. Bradford was later to become the most outstanding man in Plymouth Colony and would serve it as governor for more than thirty years. But when Brewster first met him, he was a rather sickly, intelligent boy who spent perhaps too much

The farmhouse below was built from the ruins of Scrooby manor, a landholding of the Archbishop of York. William Brewster lived at Scrooby before his departure for Holland. William's father, the bailiff of Scrooby manor, had also lived in the thousand-year-old mansion. The house was finally torn down in 1637.

William Brewster worked in Scrooby's Post House and probably attended St. Wilfred's Church (both seen at right) before he began attending Clyfton's "forward" services. Sir Edwin Sandys (bottom), a member of the London Company, was to assist the Pilgrims in getting a patent for land in the New World.

time discussing religion and reading his Bible.

Bradford was an orphan, for his father had died just after he was born, and his mother was dead by the time he was eight. For about three years he stayed with his grandfather (also named William Bradford) until the old man died in 1596. When Brewster met him, Bradford was living in the home of his uncles, Robert and Thomas Bradford, both of whom were farmers.

A young friend of Bradford's first took him to Clyfton's Puritan services at Babworth. Bradford's uncles strongly objected to the radical ideas their nephew was listening to and to the "fantasticall" radical friends he made there. They were afraid that the boy might lose the lands he had inherited and find himself in serious trouble with the authorities if he continued hearing such dangerous sermons. But Bradford was now "one of the Puritans," and neither the "wrath of his uncles, nor the scoff of his neighbors" could change him.

Bradford told his uncles that "since it is for a good Cause that I am likely to suffer the disasters which you lay before me, you have no cause to be either angry with me or sorry for me. Yea, I am not only willing to part with everything that is dear to me in this world for this Cause, but I am also thankful that God hath given me a heart so to do, and will accept me so to suffer for Him."

William Brewster was soon as fond of Bradford as if the boy had been his

own son. In later years, in Holland, Bradford lived in William and Mary Brewster's household up until the time he married. And nearly thirty years later, in his famous history of the Pilgrims, *Of Plymouth Plantation,* Bradford wrote affectionately of "Mr. William Brewster a reverent man, who afterwards was chosen elder of the church and lived with them till old age." They were lifetime friends.

A year after Bradford began attending Clyfton's church in 1603 (when Bradford was thirteen and Brewster was thirty-seven) Queen Elizabeth died. Both Brewster and Bradford may have stood beside the gates of Scrooby manor to watch the new king of England and his party of horsemen come trooping down the Great North Road.

He was James VI, King of Scotland, son of Mary, Queen of Scots. Now that Elizabeth was dead, he was journeying from Scotland to London, where he would be crowned James I of England.

Once he was upon the throne, the two nations would be united as one.

English Separatists and Puritans had some reason to hope that the new king would support their desire to reform the Church of England. For James I had been brought up a Protestant in Scotland—and Scotland had been a Protestant Presbyterian nation for more than forty years.

But Puritan hopes in England were short-lived indeed. James I proved to be a sickly, temperamental king. His politics seemed always to favor Catholic Spain, and his view of religion was even more strongly Church of England than Elizabeth's had been.

Soon after his coronation, eight hundred Puritan ministers put their names to a petition calling for a number of reforms in the Church. Known as the Millenary Petition, it asked that churchmen give up the use of ornate robes and begged the King to see to it that all preachers be well-educated

The sixteenth-century cartoon at top left shows a Puritan's view of a church trial in England. The bishop is portrayed as an ass. In the cartoon below left a Puritan minister, preaching from the Bible, is being pulled from his pulpit by "enemies of God's word."

The seventeenth-century cartoon at right shows four wrangling sects tossing the Bible (center) in a blanket. The Anabaptists were a group which did not believe in infant baptism and grew into the Baptists of today. The Brownists were the followers of "Trouble-church" Browne. Familists believed that salvation was achieved by faith alone. "Papist" was a name then used in England for Roman Catholics (followers of the Pope).

The Anabaptist.   The Brownist.

The Familist.   The Papist.

and hardworking—for some were ignorant, and many parishes went without services for long periods of time. They also asked that the Sabbath be more strictly kept.

For the past nine years Puritans had been complaining about the gay and lighthearted way in which other Englishmen were used to spending their Sundays and church holidays. In his splendid history of the Pilgrims,

Saints and Strangers, George Willison says: "The Puritans first attacked the time-honored way in which the English celebrated certain religious festivals, notably Whitsuntide [a week of holidays beginning on the seventh Sunday after Easter], at which time the wardens of the parish brewed ale to be sold in the church to raise money for various purposes."

"At these Whitsun-ales it was usual

Bradford, who was to be the governor of Plymouth for over thirty years, was born in this sturdy old house (above) in Auster-field, in 1590. Austerfield was a tiny farming village located two miles north of Scrooby.

William Bradford was only twelve when he deserted the Church of England parish church in the town of Austerfield (left), where he had been baptized, for the radical religious services of Richard Clyfton at Babworth.

for the 'wild-heads' of the parish, decked out in bright scarves and ribbons, their legs gartered with bells, riding hobby-horses and dragons, to dance into church and up the aisle, piping and playing, as the congregation climbed up on the pews to cheer and laugh at their antics."

The Puritans disapproved of such "profane" habits. They believed that Sunday should be spent in fasting and prayer, as the Sabbath had been kept by the ancient Hebrews. They spoke of the springtime Maypole as a "Stynking Idol." Some even said that for anyone to make merry on Sunday was "as great a sin as for a Father to take a knife and cut his child's throat."

These stern views of the Puritans naturally caused them to have many arguments and disputes with those who felt that Merrie England ought to

This map of England and Holland shows Hull and Boston, the two North Sea ports from which the Pilgrims made several attempts to escape to Holland. The inset map names the small, peaceful towns around Scrooby.

ATLANTIC
OCEAN

IRE

SCROOBY DISTRICT

YORKSHIRE
Doncaster
LINCOLNSH
GREAT NORTH ROAD
Austerfield
Idle R.
Bawtry
Scrooby
Harworth
Gainsborough
Blyth
Sutton cum Lound
Sturton le Steep
Ryton R.
Babworth
Worksop
NOTTINGHAMSHIRE
Tuxford

continue to be as it had always been. According to Willison, the enemies of the Puritans struck back, calling the reformers "sour, bloodless, and stony-hearted bigots without a spark of emotion in them, incapable of any warm human feeling." One playwright of the time let one of his characters speak of a Puritan as having a conscience "as hard as a pulpit."

King James proved to be sternly opposed to the hopes the Puritans had held in regard to the manner in which Sundays should be kept. In 1604, as Willison says, James I issued an order "declaring that Englishmen were not to be 'disturbed or discouraged from dancing, archery, leaping, vaulting, having May games, Whitsun-ales, Morrice dances, setting up May poles, and other sports . . . or any other harmless recreations, on Sunday,'" after church.

That same year, in answer to the petition of the 800 Puritan ministers, James called a conference at Hampton Court Palace on the Thames River southwest of London. Many Church of England ministers were present, but only four Puritans had been allowed to attend. After the King had kept the Puritans waiting several days, they were permitted to speak with him.

They asked the King to grant the Puritans of England something they called liberty of conscience. By this

they meant they wanted the right to worship God as they pleased. But King James knew that the reformers also wanted the right to elect their ministers from among their own congregations. This was similar to the system used by the presbyters (or elders) of the Presbyterian Church in Scotland.

When he heard the Puritans' request, King James flew into one of the terrible fits of rage that his court had learned to dread.

Willison describes the scene:

" 'I will none of that!' thundered James. 'A Scottish Presbytery . . . as well agreeth with a Monarchy as God and the Devill. Then Jack & Tom, &

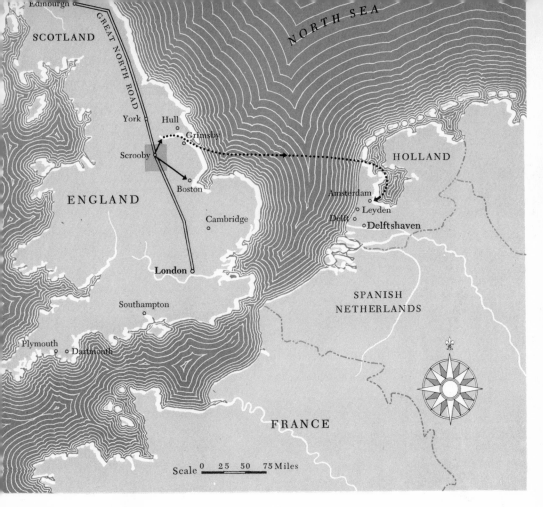

Will & Dick, shall meete and at their pleasure censure me, and my Councell, and all our proceedinges.'"

James hated anyone and anything that weakened his power. He believed in the Divine Right of Kings—the teaching that claimed that kings had been set up to rule over men by the will of God.

"Kings are not only God's lieutenants, and sit upon God's throne," said James, "but by God Himself, they are called gods."

In many ways, James was a clever ruler. He knew how dangerous it would be if he were to allow the Puritans to begin worshiping as they

chose, and to elect their own ministers. As king and head of the Church of England, he chose the bishops. The bishops, in turn, chose the ministers who preached throughout the land. Any attack on the bishops was an attack on James's royal power. If he were to allow the Puritans to question his right to govern them in religious matters, how long would it be before the Puritans began to question his right to be their king?

James had put it very simply. He said: "No bishop, no king!"

"I will tell you," James continued, "I have lived among this sort of men [in Scotland] ever since I was ten years

old, but I may say of myself, as Christ did of Himself, though I lived amongst them, yet since I had ability to judge, I was never of them.

"When I mean to live under a presbytery, I will go to Scotland again, but while I am in England, I will have bishops to govern the Church."

In a final blast at the Puritans he said, "I will make them conform themselves or I will harry them out of this land or else do worse."

To prove that he meant every word he had said, James forbade all private religious meetings and insisted that only the Church of England prayer book be used. Many Puritan ministers refused to obey the new laws. Inside of a year, three hundred preachers

The Nottinghamshire countryside of today, as seen in this photograph, looks very much as it must have appeared on the Sunday mornings when William Bradford and his friends the Brewsters walked to services at Babworth.

had been removed from their parishes.

By refusing to allow the Puritans to try to change the Church of England from within, King James made them his bitter enemies. The Puritan hatred of royal power would grow until it burst into revolution, thirty-eight years later, in the reign of James's son, King Charles I.

The Hampton Court conference of 1604 had several other important results. One of the Puritan delegates, John Reynolds, had suggested that a new translation of the Bible be made. King James agreed and set about fifty scholars of Greek and Hebrew to work under one of the most learned men in England, Bishop Lancelot Andrewes. In 1611, the Authorized or King James Version of the Bible was published. It contains some of the most beautiful English ever written and has sold more copies than any book ever printed.

This was not the Bible read by Puritans, Separatists, and Pilgrims. They preferred the Geneva Bible, which had been prepared by the Calvinists of Geneva. (The Geneva Bible is also called the Breeches Bible, for in telling the story of Adam and Eve some versions read: "and they knew they were naked, and they sewed fig-leaves together, and made themselves aprons," but the Geneva Bible reads: ". . . they made themselves breeches.")

Another important result of the Hampton Court conference was felt in Scrooby. Because of King James's new orders, Richard Clyfton chose to resign as rector at Babworth.

In 1606 the radical Brownist or Separatist congregation at Gainsborough—whose preacher now was the "forward" John Smyth — decided to split into two distinct groups. The smaller group of forty or fifty persons was to meet in Scrooby. Richard Clyfton was invited to be its pastor. Meetings had to be kept secret, because of King James's stern decrees.

It took courage to "separate" from the Church of England in 1606. The Scrooby Separatists had to risk becoming outlaws for the sake of conscience; while the less radical Puritans simply bided their time, hoping to take control of the Church and to reform it completely, at a later date, when their forces were stronger.

Brewster invited the Scrooby Separatists—or "Saints" as they now began to call themselves—to meet secretly in Scrooby manor. It is thought that they may have used the largest room in the house, which was used as the tavern. There postmaster Brewster served them refreshments free of charge, for Bradford wrote that he entertained them "with great love . . . making provision for them to his great charge."

In 1606, Mary Brewster bore a second daughter. The dangers of being a Separatist in those days may have had something to do with the name chosen for the baby, for she was called Fear.

That same year two new members—John Robinson and his wife Bridget—joined the secret group of worshipers at Scrooby manor. Both had been born in the nearby village of Sturton le Steeple. John Robinson had been a student at Cambridge, later becoming a "forward" preacher. Unlike Richard Clyfton, Robinson had been forced to leave the Church because of King James's decrees. The Scrooby meeting quickly made him their "teacher," a position second only to Clyfton's.

So Clyfton, Robinson, and the rest of the Separatists continued meeting at Brewster's each Sunday through the spring and summer of 1607; but they were not to be left in peace for long.

The Pilgrims were bewildered when greeted by scenes like this in Holland. Bradford writes: ". . . they heard a strange and uncouth language, and beheld the different manners of the people with their strange fashions. It seemed they had come into a new world."

The Flight to Holland

On September 30, 1607, William Brewster lost his job as postmaster—probably because the authorities had learned that Separatists were holding meetings at Scrooby manor.

"After these things," said Bradford, "they could not long continue in any peaceable condition, but were hunted and persecuted on every side, so as their former afflictions [troubles] were but as flea-bitings in comparison to these which now came upon them. For some were taken and clapt up in prison, others had their houses besett and watcht night and day, and hardly escaped their [the bishops' officers] hands; and the most were faine to flie and leave their howses and habitations. Yet seeing themselves thus molested, [tormented] and that ther was no hope of ther continuance ther [no hope of remaining in England], by a joynte

St. Botolph's Church is still the most impos-
ing building in Boston, as it was in 1607,
when a band of Pilgrims was taken to Bos-
ton after attempting to escape to Holland.

The Ancient Brethren had been organized in London twenty years earlier, in 1587, by John Greenwood (Penry's friend), six years before he and Penry were hanged. Some years later the Ancient Brethren relocated in Amsterdam.

Since the Ancient Brethren followed the Separatist beliefs of "Trouble-church" Browne, the Dutch called them Brownists. The people of Amsterdam speak of the street where the 300 Ancient Brethren built their new meetinghouse as the Bruinistengange (or Brownists' Alley) to this day.

Several months after William Brewster was forced to resign as postmaster at Scrooby, he and three other Separatists were made to appear before the court of the Archbishop of York—the Court of the High Commission—in the city of York. For having committed the crime of attending Separatist meetings, each of the men had to pay twenty pounds before he was freed.

Soon after Brewster's release, a majority of the Scrooby folk began selling off their property in preparation for their move. But another grave problem still stood in their way.

For the past nine years there had been in effect a law designed to stop the emigration of nonconformists (those who did not want to *conform*, by attending the Church of England). All who wished to leave the kingdom must obtain a license from the King.

The Scrooby congregation was certain that King James would never give them a permit to leave the realm. For

consente they resolved to goe into the Low-Countries, wher they heard was freedome of Religion for all men."

Clyfton's congregation must have been surprised to learn that John Smyth and his congregation of seventy or eighty Gainsborough Separatists (or Brownists) were about to leave England ahead of the Scrooby group. Soon the Gainsborough people had sold their lands and goods and had taken themselves, their wives, and their children safely to Amsterdam. There they and their pastor, Smyth, joined the Brethren of the Separation of the First English Church at Amsterdam, better known as the Ancient Brethren.

the King knew it was not likely that any nonconformist who left England would ever return of his own free will. For this reason, the Scrooby folk reasoned that they would have to slip away, illegally. And they knew that any ship captain they asked to carry them to Holland would have to be heavily bribed.

Late in 1607, Clyfton and a group of his followers (probably including the Brewsters, Bradford, and the Robinsons) started off, on foot, for the seacoast town of Boston, which lay sixty miles away to the southeast.

At Boston, plans had been laid to board a ship owned by an English captain, and to sail for Holland.

The passages that follow, quoted from Bradford's history, *Of Plymouth Plantation,* are some of the most exciting in the entire book. Except for the fact that a few phrases have been either omitted or inserted in brackets, and that spelling has been modernized,

the story reads as Bradford wrote it.

"There was a large company of them purposed to get passage in Lincolnshire, and for that end had hired a ship, wholly to themselves, and made agreement with the master [captain] to be ready at a certain day.

"So after long waiting and long expenses, though he kept not day with them [the captain did not appear on the appointed day] yet he came at length and took them in, in the night. But when he had them and their goods aboard, he betrayed them, having before complotted with the searchers and other officers [King James's local sheriff and his bailiffs] so to do; who took them, and put them [the Pilgrims] into open boats, and there rifled and ransacked them, searching them to their shirts for money, yea even the women further than became modesty; and then [the sheriff's men] carried them back into the town [Boston], and made them a spectacle . . . to the multitude,

It was down the placid River Ryton (right) that the women and children of the Pilgrim band sailed on the first part of their forty-mile journey to the seacoast town of Hull. There they were to meet the men who had traveled on foot, and the ship that was to take them over to Amsterdam.

which came flocking on all sides.

"Being thus first by the catchpole officers [bailiffs], rifled, and stripped of their money, books, and much other goods, they were presented to the magistrates [judges], and messengers sent to inform the lords of the Council of them; and so they were committed to ward [prison]."

The "Lords of the Council," whom the messengers had been sent to London to inform, were the members of King James's advisory body, the Privy Council. It then included ministers of state, archbishops, royal princes, and other advisers chosen by the King. The Privy Council probably was not very much disturbed by the news, for the Pilgrims were—to all appearances—nothing but a harmless group of country folks, after all.

"After a month's imprisonment, the greatest part were dismissed, and sent to the places from whence they came; but seven of the principals [including Richard Clyfton, John Robinson, and William Brewster] were still kept in prison and [held for trial]."

But the seven men were released soon after and never brought to trial. Then in the spring of 1608, several months after their earlier adventure, the Scrooby folk were ready to try to reach Holland again.

As Bradford tells it: "The next spring after, there was another attempt made by some of these and others, to get over at another place [near Hull, also on the North Sea coast]. And it so fell out that they [happened to meet] a Dutchman at Hull, having a ship of his own.

"He bade them not fear, for he would do well enough. He was by agreement to take them in [aboard] between Grimsby and Hull, where was a large common [or open field] a good way distant from any town."

The men were to walk the forty miles from Scrooby to the coast. The women, children, and baggage were to be put on board a bark, or barge, and sailed down "Scrooby Water," as the Ryton River was then known, into the Idle, from the Idle into the Trent, and then into the Humber, whose wide mouth empties into the North Sea.

On board the bark there may have been twenty to forty persons, including Clyfton's wife, Ann, with nine-year-old Eleazar, the youngest of her three sons; John Robinson's wife, Bridget, with their two small children, John and Bridget; and William Brewster's wife, Mary, with eight-year-old Patience and two-year-old Fear.

"But it so fell out," says Bradford, "that they [the women and children] were there a day before the ship came, and the sea being rough, and the women very sick, prevailed with the seamen to put into a creek hard by, where they lay on ground at low water [or, where they went aground at low tide].

"The next morning the ship came, but they were fast [the bark with the

When the unworldly Pilgrims arrived in Amsterdam they were upset to find it a very wealthy trading city whose busy financial life was dominated by this active stock exchange.

43

women and children was still aground] and could not stir till about noon.

"In the meantime, the [Dutch] ship master, perceiving how the matter was, sent his boat [the ship's dory] to be getting the men aboard whom he saw ready, walking about the shore.

"But after the first boat full [including eighteen-year-old William Bradford] was got aboard, and she was ready to go for more, the master spied a great company [crowd] both horse and foot, with bills [staves] and guns, and other weapons; for the country was raised to take them. The Dutchman seeing that, swore his country's oath, 'Sacremente!' weighed his anchor, hoisted sails, and away.

"But the poor men which were got aboard were in great distress for their wives and children, which they saw thus to be taken.

"It drew tears from their eyes, and anything they had they would have given to have been ashore again; but all in vain, there was no remedy, they must thus sadly part."

As for the rest of the Scrooby folk on shore, "the men that were in greatest danger, made shift to escape away before the troop could surprise them; those only staying that best might, to be assistant unto the women. But pitiful it was to see the heavy case [the

hard lot] of these poor women in this distress; what weeping and crying on every side, some for their husbands, that were carried away in the ship as is before related; others not knowing what should become of them, and their little ones; others again melted in tears, seeing their poor little ones hanging about them, crying for fear, and quaking with cold.

"Being thus apprehended [arrested by the crowd] they were hurried from one place to another, and from one justice to another, till in the end they knew not what to do with them; for to imprison so many women and innocent children for no other cause (many

of them) but that they must go with their husbands, seemed to be unreasonable . . . and to send them home again was as difficult, for . . . they had no homes to go to, for they had either sold, or otherwise disposed of their houses and livings [property].

"To be short, after they had been thus turmoiled a good while, and conveyed from one constable to another, they [the officials] were glad to be rid of them in the end upon any terms."

The men who had sailed away, "afterward endured a fearful storm at sea, being fourteen days or more before they arrived at their port, in seven whereof they neither saw sun, moon, nor stars, and were driven near the coast of Norway; the mariners themselves often despairing of life; and once with shrieks and cries gave over all, as if the ship had been foundered in the sea, and they sinking.

"But when man's hope and help wholly failed, the Lord's power and mercy appeared in their recovery; for the ship rose again.

"Fervent prayers they cried unto the Lord in this great distress . . . even . . . when the water ran into their mouths and ears; and the mariners cried out, 'We sink! We sink!' "

For the Pilgrim men, including Bradford, cried, "with . . . divine faith,

'Yet, Lord, Thou canst save! Yet, Lord, Thou canst save!'"

"Upon which the ship did not only recover, but shortly after, the violence of the storm began to abate, and the Lord filled their afflicted minds with such comforts as everyone cannot understand, and in the end brought them to their desired Haven [Amsterdam]."

The Pilgrims who had been left behind in England were still undaunted, even though two attempts to escape the country had been thwarted. Bradford concludes: "And though some few shrunk at these first conflicts and sharp beginnings, (as it was no marvel), [and although a few were discouraged by these early attempts] yet many more came on with fresh courage, and greatly animated others. And in the end, notwithstanding all these storms of opposition, they all got over [to Holland] at length, some at one time and some at another, and met together again . . . with no small rejoicing."

And indeed, by August, 1608, the last of the Scrooby Separatists—including Clyfton and Brewster, who had stayed behind to help the stragglers—had arrived in Amsterdam.

The Separatists were country people who knew no trade but farming. Naturally, they felt out of place in that great city of 240,000 people, where they had to try to learn to speak the

Cloth, which was washed after weaving, is shown stretched out to dry in the sun near Haarlem, which was, like Leyden, one of Holland's wool centers in the seventeenth century. Haarlem itself is seen on the horizon.

"uncouth" Dutch language. But in Amsterdam the Separatists had found the freedom of conscience they had striven for so many years to obtain.

At last, at the meetinghouse of the Ancient Brethren, they could attend Sabbath services openly conducted in a manner they could approve.

Nothing about their Sunday meetings suggested the Church of England. The Sabbath itself, of course, was strictly kept. Families filed into meeting in Brownists' Alley dressed in sober or "sad" colors, as the darker hues were termed. The men sat on wooden benches on one side of the aisle, the women on the other—as the ancient Hebrews had done. This custom of dividing the men and women, called "dignifying the meeting," would be continued in the New World.

Members of the congregation now lived their daily lives according to strict rules of conduct which they called the Holy Discipline of Christ. Their place of worship was always referred to as the "meetinghouse" in order to distinguish it from the churches that the Saints so heartily disliked.

Beginning at eight in the morning, on the Sabbath, the congregation stood up—sometimes for an hour—while the opening prayer was said. Kneeling was never permitted, since it reminded the people too much of Catholicism and the Church of England. There were never to be any organs in Separatist meetinghouses, either, for the same reason, and those instruments were spoken of as "the Divill's bag-pipes."

So the Psalm which followed was sung without accompaniment.

The Saints next heard a sermon, which usually lasted several hours. Their pastor might wear black gloves as well as his Sunday suit of black. When the sermon ended, another song was sung, followed by communion. Then, after a collection was taken and a benediction spoken, the congregation left the meeting for the noonday meal.

In the second service, which began early in the afternoon, there was an opening prayer and a short sermon delivered by the pastor. Then a general discussion, called "prophecying," began, in which the men might argue their opinions of a text from the Bible. The women remained modestly silent at all times, for they were not permitted to speak out at meeting.

The bishops in England mocked at the Separatist preachers of Amsterdam as "rude, mechanick fellowes." They laughed, too, to hear of their long prayers, and their "frequent and farfetcht sighes." They made fun of the short haircuts, "broad hats, and narrow ruffs" the Brownists began wearing.

But the bishops did not understand that the Separatists' democratic habits of electing their ministers and allowing the free exchange of ideas during the "prophecying" in those afternoon meetings were to have serious results in England and in America, as time would tell.

Although the Scrooby Separatists and the Ancient Brethren shared the same basic religious doctrine, heated quarrels broke out frequently between the two groups on small points of doctrine. Personal disputes also arose among them, sometimes becoming violent enough to shock the usually tolerant citizens of Amsterdam.

The Scrooby Separatists began to consider leaving Amsterdam for the beautiful university city of Leyden, which was one-third the size of Amsterdam. Some were saddened and others were angry when they learned that Richard Clyfton would remain in Amsterdam, with the Ancient Brethren.

In February, 1609, the Pilgrims sent John Robinson to Leyden, probably because his brother-in-law, John Carver, was already established there as a merchant. Soon the city authorities or burghers of Leyden granted permission for the Pilgrims—or any other persons—to settle in their city "provided such persons behave themselves."

A number of Pilgrims were apprenticed to Dutch weavers. The weavers in this seventeenth-century Dutch painting are resting beside their loom. Holland's cloth industry was carried on in the homes of the weavers.

This view (top) and map of Leyden show the Pilgrims' future home as it looked in 1614. The view depicts Leyden as a typical Dutch city, with many windmills and churches. The Pilgrims bought their pastor, John Robinson, a house in Leyden called the Green Gate. The house was on Bell Alley, near St. Peter's Church, the large building at the center of the circle drawn on the map. The Brewsters and Bradford lived within the circled area, too, on a street called Stink Alley. Robinson, who did not accompany the Pilgrims to Plymouth, died in 1625 and was buried in St. Peter's.

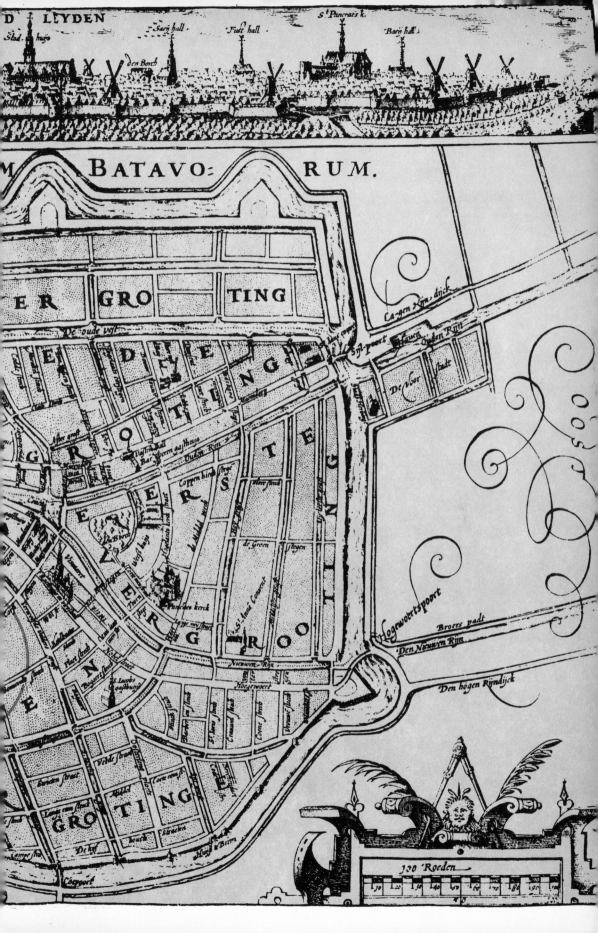

Leyden, the "Bewtifull Citie

When the authorities in England learned that Leyden was willing to admit the Separatists, the English protested to the burghers and said that the Pilgrims were fugitives from justice. But the burghers of Leyden paid no attention to their complaints.

By May 1, 1609, all of the Separatists who wanted to leave Amsterdam —numbering about 100 persons—had arrived in Leyden. William Brewster and William Bradford were among those who followed Robinson to Leyden. The Reverend Mr. Clyfton remained in Amsterdam, and so John Robinson became pastor of the new congregation.

Leyden was a center of handicraft trades. But the pride of the city lay in her great university. It was Europe's most important Protestant university and had been founded to commemorate Leyden's victory in 1574, after a Spanish siege.

The Pilgrims did their best at making a living. Since most of them were country people, they had to begin learning trades at the bottom. Bradford became a corduroy maker, and young Jonathan Brewster, who was now sixteen, became a ribbon maker. The other Pilgrims worked as wool combers and carders, silk workers, felt makers,

The Pilgrims felt much more at home in Leyden (right), with its peaceful canals and gabled stone houses, than they ever had in the large and bustling city of Amsterdam.

The document above is the official record of the civil marriage of William Bradford and Dorothy May, which they signed in Leyden in 1612. Dorothy came from Amsterdam to marry William. The signatures of the couple appear at the bottom of the certificate.

Johan van Oldenbarneveldt (below) negotiated a truce between Holland and Spain in 1609, the year the Pilgrims arrived in Leyden. Because of the truce, the Pilgrims were able to feel relatively safe in their new land.

button makers, drapers, tailors, hatters, glovers, leather dressers, cobblers, metal workers, carpenters, barbers, brewery workers, stone and brick masons, hod carriers, and printers. Eventually some of the Pilgrims were able to start small businesses for themselves, but in the beginning they were all forced to do the most lowly jobs, for other people.

It was not until May of 1611 that the Pilgrims had the time or money to set up their own meetinghouse for Sunday services. In the first years in Leyden they met in each other's houses. But in 1611 they got together enough money to buy a house called the Groenepoort (or Green Gate) in which they could hold services. The Robinsons used it as a parsonage, too.

By 1612 Bradford became a citizen of Leyden and set himself up in a corduroy business of his own. Soon after, he married Dorothy May, the daughter of Henry May, one of the elders of the Ancient Brethren in Amsterdam.

When he had set himself up in the ribbon trade, in 1617, Jonathan Brewster became a citizen.

In the years that followed the establishment of the Green Gate congregation in Leyden, its membership changed slowly. Many of the Scrooby people had remained behind in Amsterdam, while other English refugees, from other parts of the homeland, made their way to Holland and joined Robinson's church.

Although the Pilgrims never took part in Dutch political disputes and never meddled in Dutch religious debate while they lived in Holland, they knew the danger that Holland had faced in the past and was still facing during their stay there. Holland's long, bloody struggle against Spain, which had erupted in open warfare several times in the sixteenth century, was still not entirely over. Although the northern Protestant provinces of the Netherlands declared their independence from Spain in 1581, conflict had continued. William the Silent, the stadholder or chief of state of the northern provinces, was assassinated in 1584 and succeeded by his son Maurice of Nassau. Both William and Maurice had been aided in their struggle against Spain by a prominent Dutch statesman and business leader named Johan van Oldenbarneveldt.

In 1609, Oldenbarneveldt was convinced that a truce could be arranged with Spain. Maurice and the Protestant clergy did not trust Spain enough to negotiate. Oldenbarneveldt persisted, however, and in 1609 finally drew up a twelve-year truce.

This disagreement caused a split between Maurice and Oldenbarneveldt that was never mended. All through the years the Pilgrims lived in Holland, the two former allies gathered groups of supporters to combat each other's policies. Maurice had the support of Holland's powerful nobles, and Oldenbarneveldt had the support of the rich merchants and businessmen. The quarrel came to a head in 1618 when, on completely false charges of treason, Maurice had Oldenbarneveldt brought to trial and beheaded.

Many people in Holland feared the revival of open conflict with Spain when Oldenbarneveldt was executed and Maurice became more powerful. They still remembered the horror of the Spanish Inquisition when it was introduced into Holland in the 1570's with the support of the Spanish military authorities. It is possible that the Pilgrims, too, feared that war with Spain might begin again and that the Spanish and their Inquisition might come back to Holland if the truce between the two countries was broken. But the Pilgrims were largely concerned with more personal problems.

A new generation of boys and girls was growing up without memories of England. The discipline of the Separatist Church bore down hard on the spirits of the young, who watched their Dutch friends and neighbors having fun on Sundays, while they were expected to spend the day at meeting, listening to endless sermons. While their parents appreciated the skill of Elder Brewster, who was admired for "ripping up ye hart & conscience before God," many youngsters looked for jollier ways to pass the Sabbath. Necessity forced most of the young people to labor in shops and mills. Their parents, who would have greatly preferred to educate their children, grieved to watch them become "decreped in their early youth, the vigour of nature being consumed in ye very bud."

Poverty and the fear of the corruption of their youth were the chief motives by which the Separatists account for their restlessness. Their distress was increased, in 1618, by a problem involving Elder Brewster himself.

In 1617, after Brewster had at last found a means of supporting his family in Leyden by tutoring students at the university, he decided that the Separatist cause needed a press of its own. With so many Separatists in exile, there was no way to spread "ye trueth" abroad in England except through the circulation of Separatist tracts.

Brewster proceeded with caution. Together with a non-Separatist partner, he established a small printing business on his own premises. His little house was located on the Stincksteeg, or Stink Alley. In order to give his operation more tone, Brewster

The Pilgrims did not approve of Dutch celebrations like this wedding feast. It is not likely that any merrymaking would have followed the civil marriage of the Bradfords.

PERTH ASSEMBLY.

CONTAINING

1. The Proceedings thereof.
2. The Proofe of the Nullitie thereof.
3. Reasons presented thereto against the receiving the fiue new *Articles* imposed.
4. The oppositenesse of it to the proceedings and oath of the whole state of the Land. *An.*1581.
5. Proofes of the unlawfulnesse of the said fiue Articles, *viz.* 1. Kneeling in the act of Receiving the Lords Supper. 2. Holy daies. 3. Bishopping. 4. Private Baptisme. 5. Private Communion.

EXOD. 20. 7.

Thou shalt not take the name of the Lord thy God in vaine, for the Lord will not hold him guiltlesse that taketh his name in vaine.

COLOS. 2. 8.

Beware lest there be any that spoyle you through Philosophy & vain deceit, through the traditions of men, according to the rudiments of the World, and not of Christ.

MDCXIX.

William Brewster's Choir Alley press was probably smaller than the English press of 1600, above. In Leyden Brewster printed "Perth Assembly" (above left), a tract attacking King James for trying to force the Scotch Presbyterians to accept the rule of bishops. Brewster's signature is shown at left.

adopted the address of his side door, which was located on Choir Alley. The first few books to leave the Choir Alley press were inoffensive enough. But soon, strange cargo began to reach England. Concealed in the false bottoms of French wine barrels were pamphlets from Brewster's press.

Brewster printed many copies of Laurence Chaderton's 1578 attack on the Church of England. Another violent work to leave the press was the "Perth Assembly." It was this pamphlet that fell into the hostile hands of the bishops of the Church of England, and they were furious. King James demanded that the guilty printer be found and brought to him at once. He gave the job of tracking down the man

to the English ambassador to Holland, Sir Dudley Carleton. Carleton employed Dutch printers to trace the type used in the pamphlet and soon discovered that William Brewster had printed it on his Choir Alley press. Brewster's house was raided by Dutch agents. They found telltale cases of matching type in the attic, but Brewster had vanished.

In view of the hot indignation which King James felt toward Brewster's productions, it is likely that, had he been found, he would have met a very unkind fate. Another nonconformist, the Reverend Mr. Alexander Leighten, who had also published critical pamphlets abroad, was sentenced to a fine of a hundred thousand pounds. He was whipped and pilloried, had one ear sliced off, his nose split, and was branded with the letters SS (which stood for "stirrer of sedition"), and sent to London's Fleet prison for life.

The search for William Brewster went on for months on both sides of the English Channel. It occurred to many of the Separatists that as long as they remained in Leyden, their beloved elder would be a homeless fugi-

The Pilgrims must have been shocked by the pranks of the Dutch. This seventeenth-century tavern scene, painted by Dutch artist Jan Steen, shows a suitor offering his lady a fresh fish.

tive, for his family and his friends would be watched by the authorities.

The international man-hunt undoubtedly did much to turn the thoughts of the Separatists toward a new haven across the sea.

Finally, in 1617, they began to debate among themselves about where they could go to build the kind of lives for themselves that they had always wanted. They had probably read Captain John Smith's enthusiastic account of his trip to New England in 1614, which was published as *A Description of New England* in 1616. (This was the same Captain Smith who had been rescued by Pocahontas in England's ten-year-old colony at Jamestown, Virginia.) The two places most often mentioned in the Pilgrims' discussions, however, were Virginia and Guiana.

Sir Walter Raleigh wrote vividly of Guiana, on the lush, tropical northern coast of South America. He told of hidden gold, and of savages whose heads hung down beneath their shoulders. He had first visited Guiana in 1595 and in 1617 launched a second, ill-fated gold-hunting expedition into the jungle. On this trip many of his men died of fever, and he found no gold. Some of the Pilgrims, who understood nothing of the dangers of the place, however, wanted to settle in Guiana.

The Virginia colony was in trouble. Of the many hundreds of settlers who had sailed for Jamestown since its founding, most had died. Word of the hardships suffered by the Virginia colonists did get back to England, and

it had become increasingly difficult to persuade people to go to Jamestown. Without workers, the colony was a loss, both to the investors of the London Company (which had backed the Jamestown founding, in 1607) and to the Crown. A principal argument for having started the colonies was that they would provide an outlet for "this surcharge of necessitous people, the matter or fewell of daungerous insurrections." In 1616, King James had even proposed to his Privy Council that they grant reprieves to men condemned to death if they would agree instead to go to Virginia.

It was reasonable to hope that a king who was willing to send condemned men to Virginia would be willing to send Separatists.

At last, in the late summer of 1617, when the Pilgrims had decided that Virginia was definitely the place for their attempt at colonization, two representatives of the Green Gate congregation were chosen to go to England and try to get permission for a Separatist settlement. The representatives were John Carver—who was one day to be governor of Plymouth Plantation —and Robert Cushman, a deacon in the Green Gate congregation.

When they arrived in London, Cushman and Carver spoke to Sir Edwin Sandys, whom Brewster had known in Scrooby. Sandys was a member of the London Company and friendly toward the Separatists.

Sandys was greatly interested in their proposal to "plant" in Virginia

61

It is possible that this seventeenth-century Dutch painting is meant to show the Pilgrims aboard the ship (center) in which they sailed from Holland to England. The artist has painted it as a Dutch vessel, which probably bore no resemblance to the English Speedwell, *the ship in which the Pilgrims sailed to Southampton.*

with a number of families from the Green Gate congregation.

With the help of Sandys, negotiations began among the London Company, the English government, and the Separatists at Leyden for permission to settle in Virginia. The Separatists refused to discuss their religious views with the bishops of the Church of England and certainly had no intention of changing these views for the sake of gaining land. The King, after much discussion and debate, would not allow the Separatists to be given an official patent or grant of land but agreed that if they should go to Virginia "... he would ... not molest them, provided they carried themselves peaceably." This was not assurance enough for the cautious members of the Green Gate congregation.

While their letters sailed back and forth across the English Channel, some of the Ancient Brethren started off for America, after much less discussion. Elder Francis Blackwell had gathered two hundred followers for the voyage, and set sail in the fall of 1618. Their ship was blown off its course and they wandered for six months in the South Atlantic while the water supply ran low and disease broke out. When the ship finally reached Jamestown, Virginia, only fifty of the two hundred Separatists were alive. Blackwell, the captain of the ship, and all of the ship's officers were dead.

Despite their shock on hearing of the Blackwell incident, the Pilgrims were determined to go to the New World. In the spring of 1619 Cushman and Brewster went to London and finally obtained a patent. Though they were pleased with the patent, they had little faith in the freedom they would be allowed once they got to their lands. Most important of all, they could not even depend on the London Company to provide them with ships to get to Virginia. The company was near bankruptcy and would even have trouble provisioning the Pilgrims' expedition.

In 1619 a new offer was made to the Pilgrims. The Dutch New Netherlands Company, eager to build up their holdings in the New World, offered to let the Pilgrims settle in New Netherland, on the lands they claimed along the Hudson River. They offered free transportation and cattle for each Pilgrim family. In February, 1620, the Dutch company asked the Prince of Orange for two warships to protect the Pilgrims' ship on the journey to New Netherland, for they knew how greatly the Separatists feared the might of the English government. The Pilgrims liked the offer, for there they would be free of the English government and the Church of England.

Suddenly in 1620 a stranger from London—an ironmonger named Thomas Weston—appeared in Leyden with still another offer for the Pilgrims. It seemed to be the solution to all their problems. Weston told them to turn down the offer of the Dutch and to be wary of the unstable London Company. He said that he would gather a group of London businessmen who

would be willing to lend the Pilgrims the money for their transportation to the New World and for the supplies they would need. The Pilgrims could pay back the money once they were established. The idea seemed a good one to the Pilgrims, and the agreement was signed with Weston. Weston returned to London and, true to his word, gathered a group of individuals —about seventy—who wanted to invest. A joint stock company of Merchant Adventurers was formed. At last the Pilgrims were on their way to a permanent home in America.

As Bradford said: ". . . Their ends

An unknown Dutch artist painted this picture of the soberly dressed Pilgrims on the dock at Leyden, ready to board the Speedwell. *They were an anxious but hopeful band when they began the first leg of their difficult pilgrimage to a new life in America.*

were good & honourable; their calling lawful & urgente; and therefore they might expect ye blessing of God in their proceeding. Yea, though they should lose their lives in this action, yet might they have comforte. All great & honourable actions are accompanied with great difficulties, and must be both enterprised and overcome with answerable courages."

Seventy Merchant Adventurers

Thomas Weston and the Merchant Adventurers were to change the Pilgrims lives in many ways. When Weston arrived at the Green Gate in Leyden with his plans for sending the Separatists to the New World, he had convinced them to abandon the dealings they had had with both the New Netherlands Company and the London Company and to use his company of seventy Merchant Adventurers instead. Then, Weston learned that the wealthy Sir Ferdinando Gorges and a group of financiers known as the Plymouth Company had petitioned the King for the rights to Northern Vir-

London Bridge—shown here in 1639—was lined with the shops of merchants and craftsmen; it was a great trade center. The first treasurer of the group of Merchant Adventurers who financed the voyage of the Pilgrims to North America was a goldsmith whose shop was on this bridge. It is likely that other Merchant Adventurers also had businesses on the bridge.

ginia (an area extending from Pennsylvania to Newfoundland). Gorges wanted to rename the land New England. Weston knew that the King would undoubtedly issue a patent to Gorges, and so a new plan took shape.

The Plymouth Company was interested in Northern Virginia because of the rich fishing grounds that lay off the coast. There was money to be made in fishing, particularly in cod, because cod could be easily preserved by salting and drying; and codfish abounded in the waters off Northern Virginia. So the Pilgrims, Weston decided, should settle in Northern Virginia and become fishermen. Despite the fact that most of the Pilgrims were farmers with little experience in fishing, they agreed to the plan. They also liked his idea because there was no Church of England established in Gorges' territory.

The interest of Europeans—particularly Englishmen—in the northern Atlantic coast of North America was by no means new in 1620.

In 1497 John Cabot had sailed from Bristol, England, and landed on the North American continent—probably on Cape Breton Island. Although Cabot established England's claims in North America, it is quite possible that fishermen from French, Basque, and English ports had sailed to the fishing banks off present-day Newfoundland, Nova Scotia, and Maine as early as a century before Cabot.

In 1583 Sir Humphrey Gilbert began a history-making journey to the New World. He landed near present-day St. John's, Newfoundland, where he found a small settlement of fishermen. He claimed the settlement in the name of Queen Elizabeth and set up the first —although temporary—English colony in North America.

Soon after, in 1587, a group of English settlers tried to plant a second North American colony on Roanoke Island, off the coast of North Carolina.

Due to England's war with Spain in Europe, a supply ship was not able to visit the settlement again until 1591. The ship's crew found that all the settlers were gone—either killed by Indians or by disease.

England's knowledge of North America was increased greatly in 1602 by Bartholomew Gosnold who explored the Maine coast that year aboard his ship the *Concord*. Gosnold then sailed down the Atlantic coast, going as far south as Buzzards Bay on Cape Cod. Eighteen years before the Pilgrims landed at Provincetown, Gosnold had named Cape Cod and Martha's Vineyard. Cape Cod was given its name because of the quantity of cod Gosnold had seen there; for he had discovered the New England fisheries.

The English were not alone in their interest in North America. The French were soon to be established in Nova Scotia, and on the St. Lawrence. The famous French explorer Samuel de Champlain first came to Canada with a fur-trading expedition in 1603. In 1605, sailing from a French fur-trading post in Nova Scotia, he began three years of exploration, during which he charted the New England coast in detail for the first time. He sailed from Nova Scotia on the north to Martha's Vineyard on the south. He visited Mt.

The "Sacred Cod," a wood carving, hangs in the Massachusetts State House because cod fishing played so important a role in the state's history.

These workers are cleaning and drying (or "flaking") codfish. Fish were cleaned in the shed at left; then dried either on the beach or on the rack called a "stage," at right.

Desert Island off the Maine coast, mapped most of the larger rivers of Maine, and even stopped at the site of the Pilgrim's future settlement at Plymouth on Massachusetts Bay.

In 1609 Henry Hudson, sailing for the Dutch, anchored in Maine's Penobscot Bay. He later sailed south and entered both Chesapeake and Delaware bays. His most important discovery, however, was the Hudson River. For that same year he sailed up that river almost as far as the site of present-day Albany. His voyage gave the Dutch their claim to New Jersey, Long Island, and the Hudson Valley.

Sir Ferdinando Gorges, who was to play such an important part in the founding of Plymouth Colony, became interested in taking advantage of the North Atlantic's great abundance of cod and other fish shortly after Gosnold's voyage. Gorges was governor of the great fishing and trading port of Plymouth, England. In 1605 he and two other noblemen sent a navigator named George Waymouth on a voyage of exploration to the New World. Waymouth first sighted Nantucket Island. He then sailed north and landed on Monhegan Island off the coast of Maine. Waymouth stayed in the vicinity of Monhegan for more than a month, trading with the Indians and exploring the Maine coast. Waymouth and his men captured five Indians in Maine and took them back to England. Squanto, who was later to befriend the Pilgrims in Plymouth (and whose story is told here in Chapter Seven),

Sir John Popham

The French explorer Samuel de Champlain drew the map above, showing the North American coast from Cape Cod (lower left) to Nova Scotia (upper right) in 1607, the year that Gorges' expedition sailed to Sagadahoc.

Sir John Popham, although he had prosecuted Separatists as Lord Chief Justice of England, indirectly helped the Pilgrims get to the New World by joining with Sir Ferdinando Gorges (as early as 1606) in outfitting expeditions to explore the coast of New England in hope of finding sites for colonies.

Sir Ferdinando Gorges and his family were represented by the coat of arms at left.

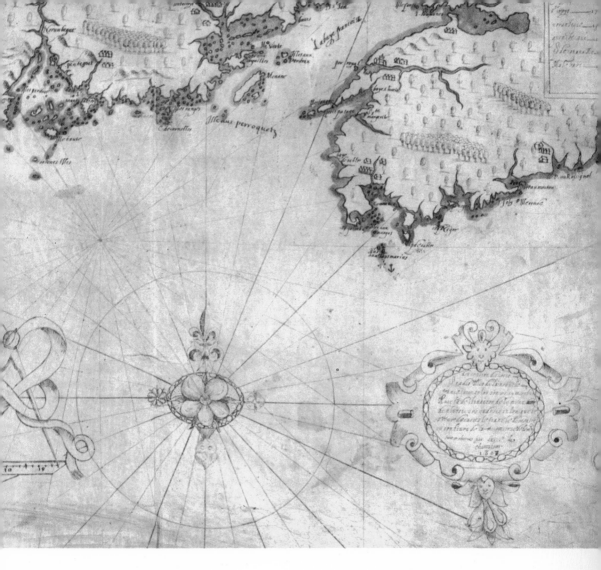

may perhaps have been one of the five.

On his return to England, Waymouth assured Gorges that Maine and Massachusetts waters were swarming with fish. Gorges was one of the most important members of the Plymouth Company when it was chartered by James I in 1606. The purpose of the Plymouth Company—as mentioned above—was to encourage and promote the founding of fishing colonies in Northern Virginia. In 1607 Gorges joined with England's Lord Chief Justice, Sir John Popham, in backing the foundation of a fishing colony at the mouth of the Kennebec River in Maine. The Sagadahoc (or Popham) colony failed in 1608, but Gorges did not give up his idea of starting a fishing empire in the New World, for he would one day ask Captain John Smith to explore the New England coast. Smith had been one of the original investors in the London Company and in 1606 sailed to the company's Virginia colony at Jamestown. When Gorges later sent him to New England in 1614 he probably asked him to establish a fishing colony there. Smith succeeded in mapping the Atlantic coastline from Penobscot Bay in Maine to Cape Cod and in loading his ship with a valuable cargo of fish and furs, but he was unable to found a colony. He did, however, give Gorges a report which the governor of Plymouth had heard before: someone *ought* to found a fishing colony on the northern Atlantic Coast; the fishing was good there.

So the Pilgrims who left their homes in Leyden on July 21, 1620, at the start of their journey to America, were meant to and indeed did fulfill Gorges' dream of establishing a permanent colony in Northern Virginia. But Gorges had yet to learn that Plymouth was never to become the base for the great fishing empire he hoped to control.

The Pilgrims must have been both a nervous and a sad company as they sailed down the canal to Delftshaven. Their understanding with Weston and his company of seventy Merchant Adventurers had never been entirely satisfactory. They would have to work very hard. For seven years a large percentage of what they earned would have to go to pay off their debt to the company—and at a high rate of interest. And the Merchant Adventurers—as the Pilgrims learned—had little interest in anything but making a profit.

The greatest cause for sadness among the Pilgrims, however, was the fact that many members of their families, for one reason or another, had to be left behind. Mary Brewster, one of the three people from Scrooby who finally sailed on the *Mayflower*, was making the journey to England with only two of her five children and without her husband William. (William was in hiding somewhere in England and was to slip aboard ship in Southampton. He had been a hunted man since he had offended the King and the bishops with the pamphlets he had printed.) Mary had her two youngest sons with her when she left Leyden: Love (probably short for Love of God), who was nine, and Wrestling (short for Wrestling with the Devil), who was six. Wrestling's name was spelled *Wrasling* in the seventeenth century, and it was pronounced that way, too. Mary had left behind her oldest son Jonathan, who was twenty-seven, and her two daughters Patience, twenty, and Fear, fourteen. The two girls were left either in their brother's care or with the Robinson family.

William and Dorothy Bradford decided to leave their five-year-old son John behind in the care of the Robinsons. They feared, perhaps, that so young a child could not survive the journey. Other men took their children and left their wives at home. A few of them took their entire families.

No matter what sadness they felt, the Pilgrims were a determined band. They had all left their homeland, England, to settle in Holland. Now they were ready to leave their adopted land behind them as well, and to set out across the Western Sea to find a New Zion—a promised land—in the wilderness.

When these drawings (above) of French ships used for cod fishing were made in the eighteenth century, many generations of French fishermen had already sailed to New-foundland and New England waters for cod.

The drawing of about 1720 below shows a large Newfoundland fishing stage. As the detailed legend at the top of the picture indicates, the valuable cod itself was dried for food; and its liver made to yield its oil.

A View of a Stage & also of ye manner of Fishing for, Curing & Drying Cod at NEW FOUND LAND.
A. The Habit of ye Fishermen. B. The Line. C. The manner of Fishing. D. The Dressers of ye Fish. E. The Trough into which they throw ye Cod when Dressed. F. Salt Boxes. G. The manner of Carrying ye Cod. H. The Cleansing ye Cod. I. A Press to extract ye Oyl from ye Cods Livers. K. Casks to receive ye Water & Blood that comes from ye Livers. L. Another Cask to receive the Oyl. M. The manner of Drying ye Cod.

The lovely city of Delft—seen here in a painting by the seventeenth-century Dutch artist Jan Vermeer—was one of the last places in Holland seen by the departing Pilgrims. For as they sailed by canal boat from Leyden to Delftshaven to board the Speedwell for the trip to England, they had to pass through Delft.

"Removall" to America

It was July 22, 1620, when the travelers finally gathered on the dock at Delftshaven. There were sixteen men, eleven women, and nineteen children —a small company, indeed, to carry the seeds of Separatism across the sea. "Truly dolfull," said Bradford, "was ye sight of that mournful parting, to see what sighs and sobbs and praires did sound amongst them, what tears did gush from every eye, & pithy speeches peirst each harte." John Robinson blessed them and with "watrie cheeks commended them with most fervente praiers to ye Lord . . . and then with mutual imbrases and many tears, they tooke their leaves one of another, which proved to be the last leave to many of them." Yet, Bradford added: ". . . they knew they were pilgrimes, & looked not much on those things, but lifted up their eyes to ye heavens, their dearest country, and quieted their spirits."

The *Speedwell*, with her cargo of

NEW ENGLAND

The most remarqueable parts thus named.
by the high and mighty Prince CHARLES,
Prince of great Britaine

THE PORTRAICTUER OF CAPTAYNE IOHN SMITH ADMIRALL OF NEW ENGLAND

Æ·tu 37·
A° 1616

These are the Lines that shew thy Face; but those
That shew thy Grace and Glory, brighter bee:
Thy Faire-Discoueries and Fowle-Overthrowes
Of Salvages, much Civiliz'd by thee
Best shew thy Spirit; and to it Glory Wyn;
So, thou art Brasse without, but Golde within.

If so; in Brasse, (too soft Smiths Acts to beare)
I fix thy Fame, to make Brasse Steele out weare.

Thine, as thou art Virtues,
John Dauies. Heref:

Edenborough

Cambridg
The Bass
Leth
St Joh
The River forth

Schooters hill
Sandwich
Dartmouth

Harington Bay

Cape Elizabeth

Ipswich
P. Kent
Snadoun hill

Beston
Poynt Sautie
Hull

Smithe Iles

SouthHampton

Bristow
Bassable
Talbotts Bay
Cape ANNA

Fawmouth
Fullerton Ils

The River CHARLES

Cary Ils
Cheuyot hills
P. Murry
London

Oxford
Poynt Suttliff
Poynt Gorge
Cape IAMES

Plimouth
Milford hauen

STUARDS
Bay
Barwick

Simon Passeus sculpsit.
Robert Clerke excudit.

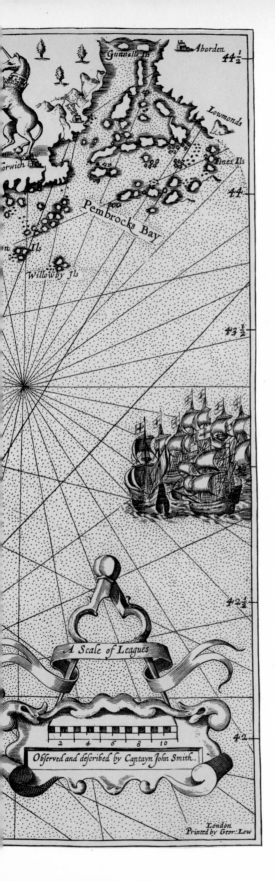

Saints, sailed first to Southampton, England, where Carver and Cushman awaited them with supplies. She was a small ship of sixty tons purchased by the Separatists in Holland. They planned to keep her in America to use as the first vessel of their future fishing fleet. As she berthed at a Southampton dock beside the *Mayflower*, the *Speedwell* must have looked extremely small.

Weston had engaged the *Mayflower* in London. She was just three times as large as the *Speedwell*, and her 180 tons were packed to the gunwales with passengers and supplies for the voyage to America. For Weston had learned of the dwindling of Separatist forces, and realizing that they could never make a successful settlement alone, he and his associates had recruited others —"Strangers," the Saints called them— to join their party. Like the Saints, they were poor people: weavers, tanners, an unemployed soldier, a few shopkeepers, a fishmonger. They came, like the millions after them, in the hope that they could build a decent life for themselves in the New World.

The two groups were almost exactly matched in number. There was, however, a third group aboard the *Mayflower:* the servants and hired men. This group was largely composed of Church of England members.

When the Pilgrims sailed for America they took with them the book John Smith wrote about his 1614 New England voyage; in it this map was included. Smith offered to accompany them, for hire, but they told him his book was "better cheap" than he.

The Strangers were Church of England people, all of them. It was an accident, a convenience, an unhappy necessity that threw them into the "holy endeavor" of the Saints. But they too proved themselves to be "pilgrimes" to the bone.

The three Strangers aboard the *Mayflower* who are among those best remembered today are John Alden, Priscilla Mullins, and Captain Miles Standish. In 1858 Henry Wadsworth Longfellow, the famous American poet, published an epic called *The Courtship of Miles Standish* in which the three Strangers were leading characters. John and Priscilla were married two years after the *Mayflower* arrived at Plymouth. Alden, who came aboard

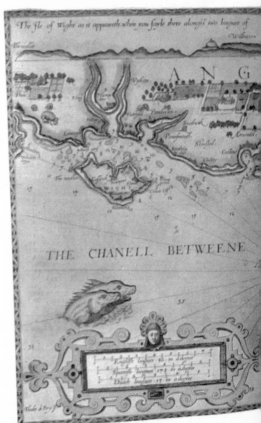

the map at top labels: Dee mill poole, Comton, Liham, Boraton Parker, Plim ton marl, The Maudlen, Lypson hill, Efford Halfe, PLIMMOVTH, the way from plimmouth to plimton marfh, the way from Plimouth to Plimſtouke, Sutton poole, cat downe, Late, Horſton paſſage, Plym roode, Plymſtouke, Fiſhers nofe, Horſtone, How Stert, Radford Hatres, Howe, the Sounde, Stodden howe

P . A . R . S

ILAND AND FRAVNCE

THE SEA COASTES OF ENGLAND betweene the Isle of Wight & Dover, with the principal havens thereof according to their situation and Appearing

Southampton, its harbor protected by the Isle of Wight, is shown in the left corner of the 1588 map at left. Here the Pilgrims from Leyden, aboard the Speedwell, met their fellow adventurers on the Mayflower, and first tried to sail for the New World. It was from Plymouth harbor—shown on the map of 1591 above—on September 6, 1620, that the Pilgrims finally sailed on the Mayflower.

as a hired man, had been a cooper or barrel maker by trade in England and was assigned the job of testing the Mayflower's barrels of fresh water, beer, and brandy for leaks during the voyage. Alden was twenty-one when he sailed on the Mayflower and was considered unusually strong. Priscilla, who was just under eighteen when she met Alden, was the daughter of a shopkeeper. Miles Standish was a seasoned

When the Mayflower *and the* Speedwell *lay at anchor in Southampton harbor, the walled port city probably appeared much as it does in this seventeenth-century print.*

professional soldier hired by Weston to lead the Pilgrims in defending their new colony. Standish had a reputation for being impatient and was often annoyed by the clumsy attempts of the Pilgrims to handle arms once they got to the New World.

There were many children aboard the ship—belonging to both Saints and Strangers—who had no idea of the great adventure they were beginning.

One little girl named Mary Allerton, the four-year-old daughter of a Saint named Isaac Allerton, lived to be the last survivor of the *Mayflower*'s passengers; she died at Plymouth in 1699, at the age of eighty-three. With Mary aboard ship were her two brothers Bartholomew and Remember, and her mother, who was also named Mary. William and Dorothy Bradford had to leave their own five-year-old son John in Leyden. Neither John and Catherine Carver nor Edward and Elizabeth Winslow, also on board, had children.

At the dock in Southampton the passengers on the *Mayflower* and the *Speedwell* made each others acquaintance quickly and immediately began discussing plans for the voyage. There was plenty of time for visiting, for hours and many days passed, with no apparent progress toward departure.

The Separatists had not been able to raise enough money to pay for all their supplies, and the investors turned down their urgent pleas for more funds. Three different men, each of them working separately, had been charged with responsibility for buying supplies. They worked at cross purposes, buying poorly, without a common plan or proper knowledge of their future needs. Brought together, there was nothing but "wrangling & expostulating" about the money. One thing was agreed. It was not sufficient.

But the greatest stumbling block arose over the contract presented by Weston. Originally, the Merchant Adventurers had agreed to permit the colonists to spend two days of every week in working for themselves. They were to own the houses and garden plots they built and tended. But when Weston came down to Southampton to see them off, he handed them a revised document. It provided that the houses and garden plots be included in company property, and that the colonists' labor be given over completely to the benefit of the company.

Some of the Pilgrims called the amended contract an insult; they said it was "fitter for theeves & bondslaves than honest men!" The wealthier men objected that if everyone had to work for the company, there was no advantage in their bringing along servants. Both Saints and Strangers flatly refused to sign the contract.

Meanwhile, the summer season was slipping away. After more scrambling for supplies and anxious negotiating, the *Mayflower* sailed out of Southampton harbor on August 5, 1620, with the *Speedwell* following in her wake. There were one hundred twenty passengers in all, and about ninety of them were on the *Mayflower*.

But there were more delays to come. The *Speedwell* began leaking like a sieve, and the ships had to turn back to England for repairs. Sitting at the dock in Dartmouth, disappointed and unnerved, the colonists saw the days run by and wondered how God would get them out of England. They made a second departure, but the smaller ship heeled so far over that her passengers clung to her sides for dear life. This time they returned to Plymouth, where they decided to abandon the *Speedwell* as unseaworthy.

There was nothing to do but to crowd everyone aboard the *Mayflower*. Twenty people stayed behind, either because they had become too discouraged to continue or because there simply was not enough room. Crowded in the 'tween decks as they were, there was scarcely room for a sigh to escape.

Cushman, who had had to stay behind, had said "if we ever make a plantation, God works a mirakle; especially considering how scante we shall be of victualls, and most of all ununited amongst our selves and devoyd of good tutors & regimente. Violence will break all."

But there was no returning, and they sailed on September 6, 1620. Fresh winds sped them from England's shore. The *Mayflower*'s seasick passengers "did cast and scour" until they grew accustomed to the ocean swell, but they made good progress westward. Soon, however, an autumn gale blew out of the north. The terrified landlubbers bumped and jostled against each other as the top-heavy ship pitched wildly from side to side. The wind shrieked in the rigging and the vessel strained and groaned, laboring through the heavy sea. At one point, one of her main beams cracked and had to be mended with a great iron screw, which one of the passengers had brought along from Holland.

In his book *The Story of the "Old Colony" of New Plymouth*, Samuel Eliot Morison, the famous American historian, explains what the *Mayflower* would have been like. She was ninety feet long and twenty-five feet wide at her broadest. The waist of the ship (the middle part of the main deck that was opened to the weather) was covered with canvas to keep salt spray from both passengers and cargo. Both the bow and the stern of the ship had high wooden superstructures. The superstructure at the stern was bigger and higher than the superstructure at the bow; for this sterncastle, as it was called, contained the great cabin where

the ships' officers ate, as well as the captain or master's cabin. Both the great cabin and the master's cabin had extra bunks built in where the more important members of the Pilgrims' company probably slept. The superstructure at the bow end of the ship— called the forecastle—contained both the crew's quarters and the galley where the crew's meals were prepared. It is likely that the Pilgrim families had to do whatever cooking they could manage elsewhere, for the galley on a ship like the *Mayflower* was small.

People grew ill and irritable in the hold of the *Mayflower*. There was little hot food, the standard fare being cold biscuit, salted beef, and beer. Everyone lived in dread of drowning, for the ship was leaky in her superstructures, and streams of icy water kept pouring in upon the Pilgrims.

Bradford tells of a narrow escape from death that one Pilgrim had during a storm at sea: "In sundry of these storms the winds were so fierce and the seas so high, as they could not bear a knot of sail, but were forced to hull [to heave to, under short sail, and drift with the wind] for divers days together. And in one of them, as they thus lay at hull in a mighty storm, a lusty young man called John Howland, coming upon some occasion above the gratings was, with a seele [roll] of the ship, thrown into the sea; but it pleased God that he caught hold of the topsail halyards which hung overboard and ran out at length. Yet he held his hold (though he was sundry fathoms under water) till he was hauled up by the same rope to the brim of the water, and then with a boat hook and other means got into the ship again and his life saved. And though he was something ill with it, yet he lived many years after and became a profitable member both in church and commonwealth. In all this voyage there died but one of the passengers, which was William Butten, a youth, servant to Samuel Fuller, when they drew near the coast."

The frequent praying and psalm-singing of the Saints had roused the Strangers to anger. Every day Elder Brewster led the daily prayers. But he was no ordained priest, nor did he read the prescribed services of the Church of England. Nor did the Leyden people confine their praying to themselves. They made it clear that they expected to impose their views on everyone, even though they numbered little more than a third of those on board.

The Strangers objected, fearing that the wrath of God would descend upon them all. And it was true enough that if the ship were to sink under the weight of Separatist sin, no distinctions could be made between Saint and Stranger. They would all drown together. But the Separatists prayed on, in spite of jeering and complaints. If mighty King James had not intimidated them, surely their present companions would not.

For sixty-six long days and sixty-six long nights they sailed westward. Some of them must have wondered if there really was such a place as America on the other side of the ocean, for there was no end to the sea.

On the morning of November 10, 1620, a pallid dawn disclosed a strip of land. Everyone rushed to the deck, craning necks and elbowing neighbors for a sight of America. There was laughter and weeping and immense

This is the departure of the Pilgrims from Plymouth as imagined by an artist of the nineteenth century. The May-flower is lying at anchor in the harbor, and the passengers are being rowed out to her in small boats as tearful farewells are said at the dock.

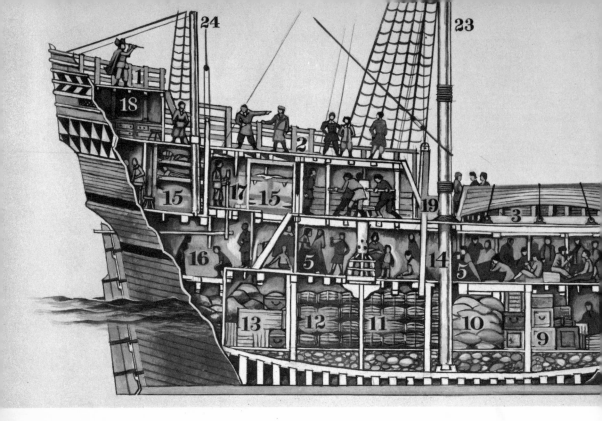

Despite all of the inconveniences of sailing on the Mayflower, the Pilgrims, at least in one way, were very fortunate passengers. The Mayflower was a "sweet" ship. She had been used in the wine trade, and her hold had a pleasant smell from the leakage of the wine casks. Most seventeenth-century ships had an overpowering smell of garbage and rotting cargo. The Pilgrims were also fortunate in Master Christopher Jones, the Mayflower's captain. He had skippered the ship for twelve years and handled her skillfully. The drawing above is a cross section of the Mayflower II, a modern attempt to re-create the original Mayflower from information available. The key below explains the drawing.

1. Poop deck
2. Quarter deck
3. Upper deck
4. Forecastle
5. Main deck (The Pilgrims lived here with most of their possessions. There were no bunks or hammocks to sleep on, so beds had to be made here or on the upper deck)
6. Crew's quarters
7. Boatswain's store
8. Galley, with cooking range
9. Main hold (containing cargo and supplies including barrels of beer, dried meat, and vegetables)
10. Cargo
11. General stores
12. Barrels of water
13. Barrels of biscuit and flour
14. Temporary cabin
15. Special cabins
16. Tiller room
17. Helmsman with whipstaff connected to the tiller (ship is steered from here)
18. Captain's Great Room or Great Cabin (in the sterncastle)
19. Pens for livestock
20. Beak
21. Bowsprit
22. Foremast
23. Mainmast
24. Mizzenmast

relief. They had sighted Cape Cod.

Captain Christopher Jones tacked south, along the outer arm of the Cape. Directly in the path of the ship lay Tucker's Terror (now known as Pollack's Rip), a boiling shallows well known to mariners, even in those days. Instead of heading his ship out to sea again to avoid the shoals, Captain Jones announced that the waters were impassable, and he returned to the northern tip of Cape Cod that night.

By morning, the *Mayflower* had anchored in the shelter of Provincetown harbor. Behind them lay a savage expanse of sea; before them, a bleak, sandy shore. There was not a house to be seen; just a few scrubby trees, bent from the wind, under a heavy gray sky.

Suddenly the rejoicing was at an end. The sailors spoke up, loud and

angry. They demanded that Captain Jones set the passengers ashore at once, and sail back to England while they still had sufficient food supplies.

And some of the Strangers said, "When they came ashore they would use their own libertie, for none had power to command them, the patents they had being for Virginia and not New-england, which belonged to another Government, with which ye Virginia Company had nothing to doe." Some historians believe many Saints and Strangers alike were surprised to find themselves at Cape Cod, as only a few Pilgrim leaders knew the *Mayflower*'s true destination.

Discontent swelled into a chorus. Mutiny was in the air. And should a mutiny break out, violence and murder might result. It was a dangerous situation, and a few of the Separatist leaders gathered in the privacy of Carver's cabin to discuss it.

It was clear that some sort of terms had to be offered to the Strangers. The servants, the hired hands, and the poorer men of both groups constituted an overwhelming majority, and they had to be reassured. It was finally agreed that a written document would be prepared, embodying the idea that everyone would have fair treatment in the government which they would set up to rule the colony.

All over the ship rival groups discussed the situation. Men hurried from one to another, arguing, compromising, amending. By the next evening, all the men had gathered in the cabin.

This photograph of the Mayflower II — a reproduction of the original Mayflower, was taken as she lay becalmed in mid-Atlantic; the Mayflower II sailed from Plymouth, England, on April 18, 1957, with a crew of thirty-three, and arrived at Plymouth

ssachusetts, fifty-four days later. The first Mayflower, carrying over three times many passengers, sighted Cape Cod in November, sixty-days after her departure September 6, 1620. Her passengers often believed they were lost on the vast Atlantic.

William Brewster, who probably drew up the document now known as the Mayflower Compact, may have been called upon to introduce the subject. Although the original document has been lost, Bradford recorded the words of the Compact as he remembered them:

"In ye name of God, Amen. We whose names are underwritten, the loyall subjects of our dread soveraigne Lord King James, having undertaken for ye glorie of God, and advancement of ye Christian faith, and ye honour of our King and countrie, a voyage to plant ye first colonie in ye northern parts of Virginia, doe by these presents solemnly & mutualy in ye presence of God, and one of another, covenant & combine ourselves togeather into a civill body politick . . . and by vertue hereof to enacte, constitute, and frame such just & equall lawes, ordinances, acts, constitutions, & offices, from time to time, as shall be thought most meete & convenient for ye generall good of ye Colonie, unto which we promise all due submission and obedience."

The reading of the Compact was followed by tense discussion. John Carver was the first to step up and sign. The leading Saints followed him. There was a long pause. Would the Strangers accept the agreement? The fate of the settlement hung on their decision.

With a rattle of his saber, Captain Miles Standish rose up to his full height and then marched to the front of the cabin and set his name down on the side of law and order. Everyone breathed easier. The most prosperous of the Strangers followed him. After them came most of the unpropertied males. And last of all came four of the servants. Women, being chattel property, and having no legal rights, were excluded.

With the unanimous election of John Carver as governor—the first popularly elected governor in the history of English colonizing—the historic meeting came to a close.

The Mayflower Compact was an extraordinary document, and it was the product of a highly extraordinary set of circumstances.

It did not alter the fact that among them some were masters and some were servants. Nor did it grant the right to participate in government to all. It excluded the unpropertied, and the women, by implication. And Plymouth's later rules of local government allowed Strangers to vote in the colony only if they had the "leave and liking" of the governor or two of his assistants.

Yet, before the Mayflower Compact, all colonists had left under sealed orders from their sponsors. Power had rested in the hands of an appointed governor, and he was responsible solely to the men whose money had been invested in his voyage. A leader had now been chosen by the men whom he was to govern, and if they did not feel he conducted the business of the colony properly, they could elect another man to replace him. The Pilgrims had dared to do what few men before them had dared—they had begun to govern themselves. By means of the Mayflower Compact they could choose their own ruler, just as they had earlier chosen their own religious leaders. No king had appointed their civil leader, and no bishop had appointed their minister.

In carrying the tradition of their church elections into their first election of a civil official, the Pilgrims established a custom that was never abandoned in Plymouth Colony—and which would have a considerable effect on the growth of democratic ideas in America. For the officers who governed Plymouth would from then on be chosen annually by direct election of those Saints and Strangers who had the right to vote.

The Mayflower Compact was to play an important part in the lives of all the Pilgrims. It is quite likely, however, that the written document did not seem half as important to them as did the fact that they had arrived safely at a place where they intended to stay. Bleak though it was, the Pilgrims must have felt great happiness when they first sighted Cape Cod and the New World; for as Bradford says: "... after long beating at sea" they had at last arrived at "that land which is called Cape Cod; the which being made and certainly known to be it, they were not a little joyful."

A modern artist painted this picture of the signing of the Mayflower Compact on shipboard off Cape Cod. The artist has tried to re-create the dark Great Cabin of the Mayflower *where the formal signing of the document probably took place.*

This nineteenth-century painting shows the Mayflower, coated with icy spray, at anchor in Plymouth harbor. A small boat loaded with Pilgrims is headed for the shore. Many Pilgrims lived aboard the Mayflower until she returned to England.

"Hard and Difficulte Beginings"

On November 11, 1620, the first party of sixteen armed men from the *Mayflower* went ashore on the tip of Cape Cod and stayed just long enough to look around quickly and to collect a load of firewood. They returned to the ship with favorable reports of the new land. They made no attempt to leave the ship on the following day—which was Sunday. On Monday, November 13, the women went ashore to do the washing that had accumulated on the long voyage across the Atlantic.

While the women washed, the men who had come with them looked over the shallop (a longboat which could be either rowed or fitted with two small masts and sails) which they had brought with them aboard the *Mayflower*. The Pilgrims had intended to begin using it immediately for exploring parties, but since it had been used as sleeping quarters for some of the Saints on the voyage across the Atlantic, its seams had opened. They began repairing it that very day.

Two days later, on Wednesday the fifteenth, an exploring party of sixteen men—led by Miles Standish and including William Bradford—went ashore. When they had gone about a mile down the beach they saw five or six Indians and a dog. When they saw the Pilgrims, the Indians quickly disappeared into the woods that fringed the beach. The Pilgrims, knowing little of the Indians' skill in moving swiftly and silently, spent the day trying to catch them—with no luck. Standish and his men spent three days ashore. They found on a hill in present-day Truro (a hill which was to be named Corn Hill) baskets of seed corn buried by the Indians. They took some of the corn back to the *Mayflower* with them when they returned.

About ten days after the return of the Standish party, the shallop had been well enough repaired to be put into use. A group of thirty-three men commanded by the *Mayflower*'s captain, Master Jones, was sent out immediately. Twenty-four of the group were Pilgrims, and nine were crewmen from the *Mayflower*. The expedition went back to Corn Hill at Truro to take more of the corn that the earlier party had found. Near the store of corn they discovered baskets of wheat and dried beans. Quantities of each were sent back to the *Mayflower*.

On December 6, the shallop set out a third time; several days later it arrived at the deserted site of Plymouth, (which Captain John Smith had named in 1614). Eighteen men were in the party, again made up of Pilgrims and crew from the *Mayflower*, including Winslow, Bradford, Standish, and Carver. They reached Clark's Island in Plymouth harbor on Saturday, December 9, and—in order to keep the Sabbath—stayed there until Monday morning, December 11. On that day the party of eighteen men stepped ashore. It is not impossible to believe—as legend has it—that they first stepped ashore on Plymouth Rock. (The landing on Plymouth Rock is now dated as having occurred on December 21, 1620. Since England and her colonies did not adopt the presently-used Gregorian calendar until 1752, ten days must be added to all dates given in Pilgrim records in order to determine the date according to the modern calendar.)

The crew from the shallop was pleased with Plymouth and thought that it would make a good place for a settlement. They sounded the harbor to see if it could accommodate ships, and when they found that it could, they started back for the *Mayflower*.

They arrived at the ship a day later to be met with sad news. While he was away, William Bradford's wife Dorothy had fallen from the *Mayflower* and drowned, although the ship had been lying quietly at anchor at the time. Many of the Pilgrims aboard the *Mayflower* were by this time terribly discouraged with the hardships of life in the New World, and it is possible that Dorothy took her own life. Had she done so, Bradford and the other Pilgrims would have considered it a

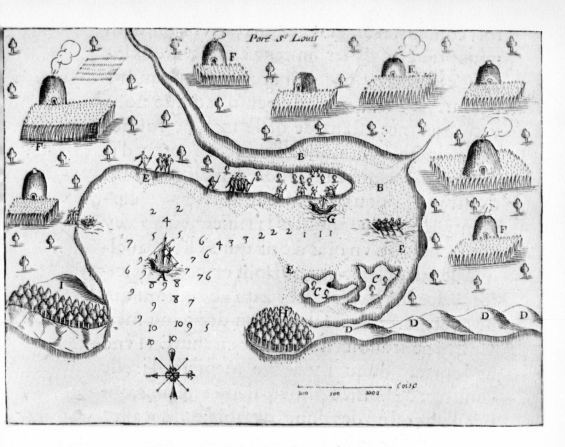

Between 1605 and 1608 Samuel de Champlain explored and mapped the New England coast. He drew this map of Plymouth harbor, which he named St. Louis for a favorite saint of France. The Indian village shown here is probably the home of Squanto's Patuxet Indians. The map was included in a book printed in 1613.

shameful and sinful act. In his diary, under the heading "Deaths," Bradford made the following notation: "Dec. 7. Dorothy, Wife to William Bradford."

The Pilgrims were happy to learn that a site for the colony had been found. After three days of debate they definitely decided to land at Plymouth. On December 16, the *Mayflower* anchored off Clark's Island to wait out the Sabbath (which was the next day). Finally, on December 20, they decided where their town was to be built.

Plymouth was a good spot for a col-

ony for many reasons. There was a fine brook and a steep hill rising sharply from the shore—a splendid site for a fort. But Plymouth had another decisive advantage. There were large cultivated areas, only recently overgrown, in which dry husks of corn still rustled in the wind. Plymouth had been an Indian village, as the Pilgrims knew from Captain John Smith's map which they had in their possession.

It was Christmas Day, 1620, when the work on the new settlement actually began. It was not a holiday, for the

Pilgrims did not believe in celebrating Christmas, or Easter, or any of the other traditional holidays observed by most Christian churches. Many of the men had already become too ill to work ashore. Gusts of snow, sleet, and rain interrupted the work, and men fell ill so suddenly that often they could not be taken back to the ship. They were lodged in the colony's first structure, the Common House, which measured about twenty feet square.

So January passed, and February. Each day others were overcome by the terrible disease (which was probably pneumonia or tuberculosis aggravated by scurvy). The living are said to have buried the dead at night in unmarked graves to hide their losses from whatever Indians might be watching.

In that dreadful first winter Miles Standish's wife Rose, and the young

Stranger Priscilla Mullins' father, mother, and brother all died of the "General Sickness," as it was called. Late in February, 1621, William White, a wool comber, died leaving his wife Susanna and two young sons, five-year-old Resolved and a baby named Peregrine. Peregrine was born aboard the *Mayflower* in Provincetown harbor; and he was to have the distinction of being the first English child born in New England.

The disease continued ravaging the Pilgrims well into March. Edward Winslow's wife Elizabeth died late in that month.

Against the terrible winter weather a half a dozen rude huts were raised. By the end of March, the last of the *Mayflower*'s passengers had lowered their bundles into the shallop and had been rowed ashore. Of eighteen married women, only five survived. Of twenty-nine unmarried men, servants, and hired hands, only ten survived. William Brewster's family was one of three that was not decreased in number by the General Sickness.

This early nineteenth-century painting, titled Landing of the Pilgrims, *shows the first boat-load of Pilgrims debarking from the* Mayflower *on December 18, 1620. There is no evidence that they landed on Plymouth Rock, and they were not to see Indians at Plymouth for another three months. The photograph at right pictures Plymouth Rock today.*

A strange event occurred on March 16, 1621, during a business meeting in the Common House. An Indian brave marched into the settlement and would have come into the Common House, had not the sentries stopped him.

"Welcome," he said to the astonished settlers. "I am Samoset." He was an Abnaki, from Pemaquid Point in Maine. He had sailed with English captains along the Newfoundland coast, and had learned their tongue.

Samoset told the Pilgrims many things about the region in which they had chosen to live. There had once been an Indian village at Plymouth. It had been called Patuxet. In 1617 a great plague had swept the village, and all the inhabitants had died.

He also told them that the most powerful Indian chief of the area was a man named Ousamequin ("Yellow Feather"), usually called Massasoit ("Big Chief"). Massasoit was chief of the Wampanoag and lived at Sowams on Narragansett Bay, about forty miles southwest of Plymouth.

Samoset talked with the Pilgrims well into the night. After spending the night at Plymouth he left them, saying he would return the next day with other Indians and with trade goods. Samoset was as good as his word and did come back the next day with five braves, each carrying a deerskin. They also brought three or four beaver skins. The Pilgrims were impressed with the beaver skins and wanted more. Beaver was the most valuable of all furs and would bring high prices in England. Samoset sent the five braves back to Sowams for more skins and stayed behind with the Pilgrims.

When the braves had not returned in four days, the Pilgrims sent Samoset to find them. During Samoset's absence the Pilgrims had two or three scares—Indians sneaking about Plymouth making faces and rude gestures at them. Then, almost as suddenly as he had come the first time, Samoset reappeared with a friend named Tisquantum, or Squanto. To their amazement, the Pilgrims discovered that this Indian, too, spoke English.

Strange as Samoset's story may have seemed to the Pilgrims, it was exceeded by the tale told by his friend Squanto. Squanto was the last surviving member of the Patuxet tribe which had lived on the site of Plymouth.

He may have been captured by Captain Waymouth, who was then in

After 1622 religious services were held in the fort at Plymouth—shown here in a photograph of the modern restoration—until 1649, when the first meetinghouse was completed.

On January 21, 1621, the Pilgrims came ashore from the Mayflower *and held their first relig-ious services on American soil (above) in their newly completed Common House, the first build-ing they put up at Plymouth. The twenty-foot-square thatched building probably bore little resemblance to the large structure the nineteenth-century artist has painted in this picture.*

the employ of Sir Ferdinando Gorges, and brought, with four other Indians, to Plymouth, England. In that event, Squanto may have lived with Sir Fer-dinando for a long time, long enough to have taught that Englishman his native language and to learn English himself. Squanto would have been a valuable prize, for from him Gorges could have learned much about New England. The young Indian could have told him which crops grew best there, how far the coastal rivers ex-tended inland, and what game was abundant, and he could have further convinced Gorges that a fishing em-pire could be built on the coast of New England.

Some think that Squanto recrossed the Atlantic with Captain John Smith in 1614, when Gorges sent Smith to America.

On this 1614 voyage, Smith was ac-companied by another captain, named Thomas Hunt. Hunt had stayed on the coast to fish, after Smith had set out

This modern painting shows the Indian Samoset greeting the surprised Pilgrims—in their own language—at Plymouth, in March, 1621. It was Samoset who told them of Squanto —another Indian who could speak English.

for home. With his ship full of cod, he sailed to Cape Cod. There he raided a Nauset village and captured about twenty Indians—one of whom was Squanto! Then Hunt clapped all of them in the hold and carried them off to Spain, where he sold them as slaves.

Squanto was purchased by some Spanish friars, "that so they might nurture [him] in the Popish religion," and convert him to Catholicism. He later managed to escape to England, where he lived for several years in the home of John Slanie, who was treasurer of the Newfoundland Company. Squanto probably returned to America on one of Slanie's ships, for he was

next heard from in Newfoundland, where Captain Dermer, another of Gorges' men, met him in 1618. Dermer took Squanto with him on a voyage to the Massachusetts coast. How joyful the twice-kidnapped Indian must have been to be at home once more!

But his joy quickly turned to grief when he witnessed the tragedy which had befallen his people. All had perished in the great plague. When Squanto learned that he was the last and only surviving member of the Patuxet tribe, he went to Massasoit at Sowams. Massasoit took him in.

The Pilgrims, for their part, soon recovered from their surprise in gaining the friendship of an Indian who knew their homeland. Squanto was to embrace the Holy Discipline and would fully deserve to be numbered among the Saints. He was, in Bradford's words, "a speciall instrumente sent of God for their good beyond their expectation."

Shortly after his arrival, Squanto's skills as an interpreter and negotiator were called into play. On March 22, 1621, Chief Massasoit, accompanied by sixty of his braves, appeared at Plymouth. They were an impressive delegation and conducted themselves with great dignity and formality. To meet them, Captain Standish hurriedly assembled his own little force, arrayed in as much steel and armor as he could muster. When they sat down to talk, there were many issues outstanding.

The Indians had good reason to want to be rid of the English. For years English sea captains had robbed them, kidnapped their young men, and killed their people senselessly with their "firesticks." The Indians suspected, and perhaps correctly, that the English ships had brought the terrible plague to their land.

One advantage the Pilgrims had in the negotiations was something of which they were unaware. The Wampanoag were often at war with a neighboring Indian federation known as the Narragansett. The English would be useful allies for the Wampanoag if they were attacked by the Narragansett. Squanto used this fact in helping to negotiate a peace treaty between Massasoit and Governor Carver.

It provided that the Indians would return a number of metal farming tools which they had taken from the colonists a few weeks before, and the Pilgrims would in turn pay the Pamet Indians for the seed corn the Pilgrims had taken during their first explorations on Cape Cod. Each group would punish any of their own people who might offend the other. Neither would go to the other with weapons in their hands. And, if a third group were to make war upon either side, the other would come to the aid of the party under attack.

It was a fair treaty. It reflected the fact that the Indians and the English were then nearly equal in power. Because it was fair, it endured for more than fifty years. The Indians left, satisfied, on March 23, 1621. Squanto remained behind to help the Pilgrims.

Squanto, shown above as a modern sculptor imagined him to be, was a true and helpful friend of the Pilgrims. Once Samoset had introduced him to the Plymouth settlers, Squanto never left their side, for he adopted their religion. Massasoit, seen below in a modern statue, signed a peace treaty with the English settlers who had built their homes on his land. A member of the Mayflower's crew remembered Chief Massasoit as a "very lustie man in his best years."

According to their Old Style calendar, the Pilgrims' New Year's Day fell on March 25. This was the day when they had to elect their governor for the coming year. John Carver was re-elected.

On April 5, a sober day in the lives of the Pilgrims, the *Mayflower* sailed for England. Her hold was empty. The sailing must have left them all with two sober thoughts: they were at Plymouth to stay, no matter what happened; and they had already fallen behind in paying off their debt to the Merchant Adventurers in London.

The misgivings of the Pilgrims were undoubtedly increased when, about a week after the *Mayflower* sailed, their leader John Carver died suddenly while planting corn in the fields.

Around the middle of April, Plymouth's voters met and elected William Bradford governor, and Isaac Allerton, the father of little Mary Allerton, was made Bradford's assistant.

As the spring progressed, the Pilgrims learned more and more from their friend Squanto. He taught them to plant corn—four kernels to the hillock, in true Indian fashion. He showed them how to catch herring from Plymouth's Town Brook for use both as food and as fertilizer; he also showed them how to tap maple trees for their sweet sap and where to find fat eels.

The Pilgrims held their first Thanksgiving feast in mid-October, 1621. The modern picture at left shows one of the five roasted deer (upper left) that were served. Only a few of the ninety-one Indian guests are seen.

101

Squanto probably taught them some of the typical Indian techniques for trapping deer and other game, as well.

This first spring brought one event which did not involve farming. Edward Winslow had lost his wife Elizabeth in the General Sickness of the winter; and Susanna White, the mother of Resolved and Peregrine, had lost her husband. They decided to get married. Governor Bradford performed a civil wedding ceremony for them on May 12, 1621—since the Pilgrims did not believe that weddings were in any way religious. The Winslow wedding was the first wedding to take place in New England.

The colony began to thrive during its first summer. The Pilgrims, who had feared for their very lives in the cold of the cruel winter, were now seeing the best of the New World to which they had come. Corn ripened in the fields. Grapes grew warm in the sun.

During the summer, the Pilgrims sent the shallop into the vicinity of what would one day be Boston harbor, to trade for beaver pelts with the Massachusetts Indians.

The Pilgrims' first autumn in New England was beautiful and the harvest of Indian corn was plentiful. The Pilgrims were thankful for their survival and decided to set aside a day of Thanksgiving for a harvest festival.

Bradford probably named a day in October for the celebration of the first Thanksgiving. The Pilgrims and their descendants often observed it during the years ahead. America's present-day celebration of Thanksgiving in November was established by President Abraham Lincoln, who first made it an official national holiday in 1863.

For the Pilgrims' Thanksgiving Day Bradford dispatched Squanto to Sowams, to invite the Wampanoag braves to the feast. Four men were sent out to shoot waterfowl, and they returned with enough ducks and geese to keep

RELATION OR
Iournall of the beginning and proceedings of the Englifh Plantation fetled at *Plimoth* in N E W ENGLAND, by certaine Englifh Aduenturers both Merchants and others.

With their difficult paſſage, their ſafe ariuall, their ioyfull building of, and comfortable planting themſelues in the now well defended Towne of NEW PLIMOTH.

AS ALSO A RELATION OF FOVRE
ſeuerall diſcoueries ſince made by ſome of the ſame Engliſh Planters there reſident.

I. In a iourney to PVCKANOKICK the habitation of the Indians greateſt King Maſſaſoyt : as alſo their meſſage, the anſwer and entertainment they had of him.
II. In a voyage made by ten of them to the Kingdome of Nawſet, to ſeeke a boy that had loſt himſelfe in the woods : with ſuch accidents as befell them in that voyage.
III. In their iourney to the Kingdome of Namaſchet, in defence of their greateſt King Maſſaſoyt, againſt the Narrohiggonſets, and to reuenge the ſuppoſed death of their Interpreter Tiſquantum.
IIII. Their voyage to the Maſſachuſets, and their entertainment there.

With an anſwer to all ſuch obiections as are any way made againſt the lawfulneſſe of Engliſh plantations in thoſe parts.

LONDON,
Printed for *Iohn Bellamie*, and are to be ſold at his ſhop at the two Greyhounds in Cornhill neere the Royall Exchange. 1622.

In 1622 a book known as Mourt's Relation *was published in London. Its title page is shown at left. It told of the delights of living in Plymouth—of its "joyfull building," and its "comfortable planting" (see page 105). The book was intended to attract more settlers to Plymouth, then dangerously short of manpower and fighting off starvation.*

Peregrine White, the first English child born in New England, slept in the cradle at right. His name, Peregrine, comes from the Latin word signifying "stranger"—from which the word "pilgrim" (one who makes a pilgrimage or foreign journey to a shrine) is also derived. Peregrine lived to be eighty-four. William Bradford's signature (below) is seen over a page in his treasured Geneva Bible.

the company for a week. They probably shot wild turkeys as well, for they were plentiful in the country about Plymouth. In every household, preparations were under way.

The appointed day was at hand, golden and resplendent. It was noon when Massasoit arrived, with ninety hungry braves. The Pilgrims were appalled by their number. They could never feed them all. Massasoit read the concern upon their faces. With a simple gesture, he dispatched a few of his men into the forest. Soon after, they returned, bearing five deer as their contribution to the feast.

Goose and venison, lobster, eel pie, corn bread, fresh "sallet herbes," wild plums, berries, and red and white wines were served. The Indians enjoyed themselves so much that they stayed for three days.

A warm October sun enveloped the harvest scene, shining equally on the Pilgrims who had set their feet upon a strange new land, and upon the Indians who had made them welcome.

Plymouth Plantation

Although the Pilgrims had given thanks for the harvest of 1621, the tiny settlement (containing about sixty persons) was still nothing but a line of rude, thatched huts strung along Plymouth's Town Brook. Their nearest English neighbors were either hundreds of miles away in the temporary, scattered fishing villages on the coast of Maine, or to the south in Virginia.

Farther north, in Canada, were the hostile French. The Dutch had built a trading post at present-day Albany, in 1614, and claimed the lands surrounding New York harbor and the Hudson River. England lay two to four months away on the other side of the wintry gray waters of the Atlantic. To

A copy of the seal of Plymouth Colony is shown above. The original was probably sent over from London by the Merchant Adventurers in 1624, for use on official documents.

the west, behind them, were the forests of wilderness New England. Ringed about by Indians—Pamet and Nauset on Cape Cod, Wampanoag and Narragansett to the south and west, and the Massachusetts to the north—the Pilgrims must have looked anxiously to Captain Miles Standish, wondering if he could save the colony if it was attacked.

On November 11, 1621, just a year after the *Mayflower* first anchored off Cape Cod, the Pilgrims sighted a ship coming into the harbor at Plymouth. It proved to be the fifty-five-ton *Fortune,* which had sailed from London four months earlier, in July. On board were thirty-five men, women, and children who had come to live in Plymouth. Elder William Brewster was no doubt overjoyed to see his twenty-eight-year-old son, Jonathan. Edward Winslow welcomed his younger brother, John; and the entire band of Saints must have gathered to greet their former deacon from the Leyden congregation, Robert Cushman. With Cushman was his fourteen-year-old son, Thomas, and the nineteen-year-old French-speaking Walloon, Philip De La Noye (an ancestor of President Franklin Delano Roosevelt).

The *Fortune* also carried several important papers. The first was a patent, signed by Sir Ferdinando Gorges and the other members of the new Council for New England (the reorganized Plymouth Company). It promised the Pilgrim settlers 100 acres of land apiece at the end of seven years.

The second was an angry letter from Thomas Weston, asking the Pilgrims to copy out and sign their contract with the Merchant Adventurers—for the Separatists had refused to put their names to any agreement before the *Mayflower* sailed. Weston also complained that no cargo had returned to England in the *Mayflower.* "That you send no lading in the ship is wonderfull," Weston wrote, "and worthily distasted. I know your weaknes was the cause of it, and I beleeve more weak-nes of judgmente, than weaknes of hands. A quarter of the time you spente in discoursing, arguing and consulting, would have done much more, but that is past," his letter continued.

Weston's letter also told the Pilgrims that unless the contract was signed, they could expect no more money and supplies from London. After Deacon Cushman preached a sermon on "The Dangers of Self-Love," urging the Pilgrims to sign, they stepped forward and put their names to the agreement with the Merchant Adventurers.

In these early years in New England, fish, furs, and lumber were the only valuable goods the Pilgrims could use in paying off their debt. Although they were to try to set up fishing stations on Cape Ann, the Pilgrims would never have much success as fishermen. But they had already begun cutting cedar logs and splitting them into clapboards; and beaver trade with the Indians had been started.

When Deacon Cushman left Plymouth a month later, in December, the hold of the *Fortune* was laden with cedar clapboards and several kegs of beaver pelts worth about 500 pounds—nearly half the amount owed to the London merchants. Also on board, in Cushman's possession, was a manuscript written by Edward Winslow and Governor William Bradford. It told the stories of the Pilgrims' first "discoveries" on Cape Cod, the visit of Massasoit, and the first Thanksgiving.

Just as the *Fortune* reached the English Channel, she was captured by a

French privateer and robbed of all her cargo. The French finally allowed the ship to sail to London, where Cushman informed Weston of the loss. Cushman then delivered the Bradford-Winslow manuscript to a printer named John Bellamie, who published it in 1622 under the name of a mysterious "G. Mourt." For this reason, it is known as *Mourt's Relation,* and was the first printed account of the early settlement of Plymouth to be read by the public in England.

Soon after the *Fortune* sailed away, Plymouth Colony was alarmed by the threat of war with the Indians. Canonicus, chief or sachem of the Narragansett, sent Governor Bradford a sheaf of arrows wrapped in a large snakeskin. It was a challenge to battle. Bradford returned the snakeskin stuffed with bullets.

Fortunately, Canonicus did not attack the settlement. But his challenge caused the Pilgrims to begin building a "strong pale," or palisade, around their village. It took them four months to complete the eleven-foot-high enclosure, for it was almost a mile in circumference. They worked every day except the Sabbath—even including Christmas Day, 1621—until the next spring when the gates and walls were finished.

In March, 1622, red-haired Miles Standish set out in the shallop on another beaver-trading expedition to the Massachusetts Indians, taking Squanto and another trusted Indian companion, Hobomok, with him. They had "good

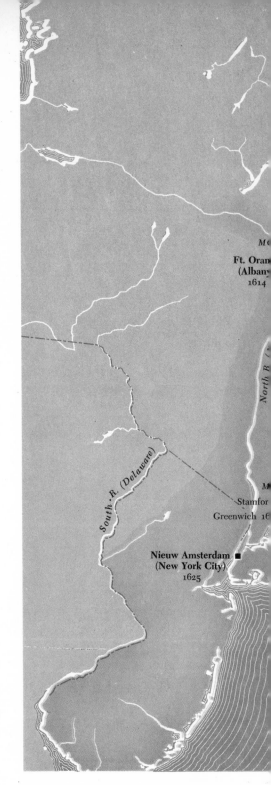

ABNAKIS

Pentagoet (Castine)

Kennebec

PLYMOUTH
COLONY
TRADING
GRANT
1628

Sagadahoc   ○ Monhegan Island

Varsche R. (Connecticut)

○ Naumkeag (Salem) 1626

Mt. Wollaston   ○ **Boston** 1630
(Merry Mount) 1625   ○ Wessagusset (Weymouth)
1622
MASSACHUSETTS   OLD COLONY LINE 1642
NIPMUKS

Matianuck (Windsor)
○ 1633

Providence   **PLYMOUTH**   ○ **Plymouth**
1636 ○   **COLONY**   1620
■ **Ft. Good Hope**   *WAMPANOAGS*
(Hartford)   Aptucxet
sfield ○   1633   △ Sowams   ○ 1626   ○ Barnstable 1639
△ Mt. Hope
NAUSETS
pac
aven)   *MOHEGANS*
-8   ○ Guilford   *PEQUOTS NARRAGANSETTS*
○ 1639
d   ○ Saybrook 1635

Atlantic Ocean

**EARLY SETTLEMENTS
OF THE ENGLISH AND DUTCH
IN NEW ENGLAND**

■ DUTCH SETTLEMENTS   △ INDIAN SETTLEMENTS
○ ENGLISH SETTLEMENTS   ☐ DUTCH CLAIMS PRIOR TO 1650
☐ PLYMOUTH COLONY PRIOR TO 1692

Scale 0   10   20   30 Miles

*The above map locates some of the towns founded in New England by Plymouth's Pilgrims
and the Puritans of Massachusetts Bay, as well as Plymouth's important beaver trading
posts at Aptucxet, Matianuck, and Pentagoet, and on the Kennebec River. The inset
shows the earliest known view of the Dutch settlement on Manhattan Island in New York.*

107

Myres Standish

The above portrait of Miles Standish may not be genuine, but his sword and signature, shown below it, are known to be authentic.

The picture of Edward Winslow at left is the only authentic portrait in existence of any of the Mayflower Pilgrims. It was painted in 1651, when Edward and his son Josiah were in England. Winslow first joined Brewster as a printer at the Choir Alley press in Leyden, and probably was not a gentleman of "qualitie" as was later claimed. Nevertheless, the Winslow coat of arms (above, left) is thought to have been displayed in 1680 at Josiah Winslow's funeral in Plymouth.

trade, and returned in safety, blessed be God," said Bradford.

Since Weston sent no supplies, the colony grew desperately short of food during April, May, and June. By the middle of summer, two of Weston's ships—the *Charity* and the *Swan*—arrived in Plymouth. They put ashore about sixty of Weston's men, with not so much as a "bite of bread," said Bradford. Also aboard was a letter from Weston to Bradford. Weston said that he was no longer one of the Merchant Adventurers. Plymouth could expect no more help from him. "I am quit of you," said Weston, "and you of me, for that matter."

Weston also asked Bradford to feed his sixty men until they could set up their own rival post to trade with the Indians. Although they were living from hand to mouth themselves, the Pilgrims shared their food with the new group. Starvation was so close at hand that all supplies were kept under guard, and more than once men were 'well whipt" for stealing the corn that ripened in the fields.

That summer they heard of the "great massacre in Virginia." Chief Opechancanough of the Pamunkey Indians had risen against the English there and killed 350 people. The Pilgrims must have wondered when their turn would come, for it was during this summer that they began building a stout fort on the hill behind the village.

The ship that brought the news from Virginia to Plymouth later accompanied Edward Winslow to Maine. He sailed there in the Pilgrims' shallop, traded for as much food as he could for the starving colony, and returned to Plymouth as soon as possible.

Plymouth's second wedding occurred during the difficult summer of 1622. It was the famous marriage of tall, blond, twenty-three-year-old John Alden to the twenty-year-old orphan Priscilla Mullins. Afterward, the couple lived many years in Plymouth, before moving to Duxbury. Priscilla bore eleven children, and had been John's wife for sixty-three years when she died in 1685. Alden died the following year. If Priscilla had ever been courted by Miles Standish, the records make no mention of it.

In the fall of 1622, Weston's men left Plymouth and moved forty miles north, to a place called Wessagusset, where the town of Weymouth stands today. There on Boston Bay they set up a trading post and began "trucking" or trading trinkets to the Massachusetts Indians in return for beaver.

Since the fall harvest was poor, both Plymouth and Wessagusset found themselves facing another hungry winter. Even though the Pilgrims were now competing for beaver with Weston's men, they decided to make a joint trading expedition to the Indians to obtain food. Wessagusset supplied the ship *Swan,* and a party of men from the two colonies (including Bradford and Squanto) sailed around Cape Cod to Monomoy and bartered for supplies of dried beans and corn. On this trip, Squanto fell ill of a violent fever and died. Bradford then returned to Plymouth and traded further with the Indians in "inland places, to get what he could . . . which did help them something."

Food proved to be in even shorter supply in Wessagusset that winter than in Plymouth. In February, 1623, Wessagusset's Governor John Sanders sent a messenger to Bradford saying that the Massachusetts would not allow him to "borrow" any more corn. Sanders "desired advice whether he might not take it from them by force." Although the Pilgrims told Sanders he must by no means lay hands on the Indians' supplies, one of the Wessagusset traders had already told the Massachusetts what Sanders had been planning to do.

Soon all the tribes on Cape Cod and in the neighborhood of Plymouth knew the story. Plymouth was afraid that she might be blamed for what Sanders had thought of doing, for as far as the Indians were concerned, Plymouth and Wessagusset had been settled by the same people.

The Pilgrims claim that Miles Standish had heard Wituwamat, a Massachusetts Indian brave, threaten to ruin the Wessagusset colony. Plymouth also knew that Sanders' men had no guns. In March, Bradford sent Standish and Hobomok and eight heavily armed

men to Wessagusset in the Pilgrims' shallop. They were to pretend that they were on a trading expedition.

Some historians say that Bradford genuinely believed that an Indian uprising—like the one in Virginia—might develop if Weston's men were allowed to continue dealing with the Massachusetts, and that both Plymouth and Wessagusset might be wiped out.

Others believe that the Pilgrims invented stories about the Indian danger in order to excuse their destruction of Weston's colony. For, as Weston was now a rival, Plymouth no doubt feared that she might lose all her beaver trade to his post at Wessagusset.

This photograph of the modern restoration of Plymouth shows the town as it appeared in 1627. The main street was renamed Leyden Street in the nineteenth century — in memory of the Pilgrims' stay in Holland.

At Wessagusset, hot-tempered Miles Standish singled out the key figures among the Massachusetts braves. Without any warning, Standish and his men stabbed three Indians to death —including Wituwamat. Then, after Weston and Standish's men had killed three more and hanged a fourth, they drove the rest of the Massachusetts from their village and into a swamp.

Next, Weston's men sailed away in the *Swan,* hoping to find their leader at one of the English fishing stations on the coast of Maine. Wessagusset had been destroyed.

Standish cut off Wituwamat's head, sailed back to Plymouth in the shallop, and placed the bloody trophy on a spike on top of the fort.

The Pilgrims' former pastor in Leyden, John Robinson, later learned what had happened and wrote Bradford a letter which arrived in 1624. Robinson said Bradford should have allowed only one or two of the Massachusetts to be slain, to bring "punishmente to a few and the fear to many." Robinson also added: "Oh! how happy a thing had it been, if you had converted some, before you had killed any."

Former Merchant Adventurer Thomas Weston himself arrived in Plymouth in April, on the *Paragon,* to find out why his colony at Wessagusset

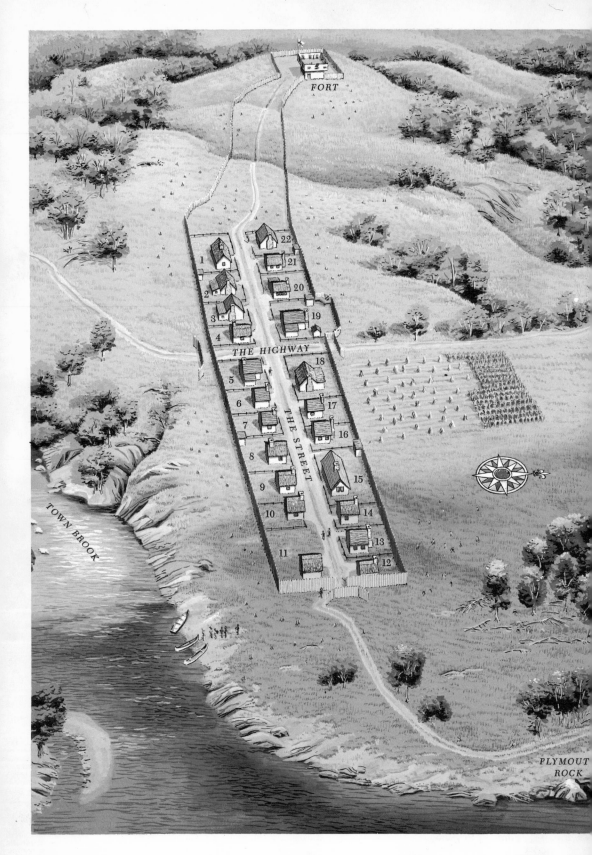

FORT

1
2
3
4

THE HIGHWAY

5
6
7
8
9
10
11

THE STREET

22
21
20
19

18
17
16
15
14
13
12

TOWN BROOK

PLYMOUTH ROCK

had been destroyed. Bradford said that "former things" were "boyling in his mind" but that Weston kept his anger in and asked them to set him up once more as an Indian trader. Since Weston had fallen into the hands of Indians in New Hampshire and lost all his trade goods, the Pilgrim leaders took pity on him and secretly lent him a small supply of beaver.

Three months later, in July, 1623, two ships arrived from England—the *Anne* and the *Little James*—carrying ninety-three settlers. The new arrivals nearly doubled the size of the little colony on Town Brook.

Among the company on the two ships were Roger Conant, who was to found the town of Naumkeag (Salem) three years later; and a girl named Barbara, who was very soon to marry Captain Miles Standish. Nothing further is known of Barbara except that she bore Standish four sons. Legend says that she was the sister of Standish's wife Rose, who had died two years before in the General Sickness.

The Brewster family must have rejoiced to be reunited, at last, after three years of separation; for twenty-three-year-old Patience and seventeen-year-old Fear had arrived to join their parents and their three brothers.

The new arrivals took one look at the Old Comers (as the *Mayflower* and *Fortune* people soon came to call themselves) and were amazed to see their "low and poore condition ashore." The Plymouth people were "ragged in apparell, and some little better than halfe naked." "Some [of the newcomers] wished themselves in England againe," said Bradford, "others fell a-weeping, fancying their own miserie in what they saw now in others; [still others pitied] the distress they saw their friends had been long in, and still were under; in a word, all were full of sadnes."

After six weeks, however, the newcomers had grown used to life in Plymouth. When the *Anne* sailed home for England, loaded with furs and clapboards, Edward Winslow sailed with her. He was going to London to try to obtain the promise of more supplies for Plymouth, and he took with him the manuscript copy of a pamphlet he had written, titled "Good Newes from New England," which included his version of what had happened at Wessagusset. Six months later, in March, 1624, he returned to Plymouth on the *Charity*, bringing a bull and three cows

his modern sketch of Plymouth shows the town in 1627, when it held less than 200 ersons. The houses shown were occupied by the families of 1, Josiah Winslow; 2, Fran-'s Cooke; 3, Isaac Allerton; 4, John Billington; 5, William Brewster; 6, Jonathan Brewer; 7, Thomas Prence; 8, Peter Brown; 12, Nicholas Snow; 13, Francis Eaton; 14, eorge Soule; 15, Richard Warren; 16, Dr. Samuel Fuller; 17, John Howland; 18, Stehen Hopkins; 19, Governor William Bradford; 20, Degory Priest; 21, John Alden; 22, aptain Miles Standish. Numbers 9 and 10 were common houses; number 11, a storeuse. The palisade was finished in March, 1622; the fort was built the following summer. By 1643, Plymouth Colony held 3,000 persons, and other towns had been founded.

—the first cattle the Pilgrims had seen since they left Europe.

That same year saw two of Elder Brewster's children wed—Jonathan marrying Lucretia Oldham, and Patience marrying Thomas Prence.

The widower Governor William Bradford was married that year to Alice Southworth, a widow with two small children—Thomas and Constant. The Bradfords later had four children of their own.

Edward Winslow was again sent to London to deal with the Merchant Adventurers, whom the Pilgrims now owed 1,400 pounds. The debt never grew smaller. The worth of the supplies sent back to Plymouth somehow always exceeded the value of the clapboards, the otter, and the beaver shipped off to London.

In 1625, Miles Standish sailed to

The photograph below shows a modern restoration of Aptucxet built in 1626, on Buzzards Bay, for use in the Pilgrims' beaver trade with the Wampanoag and Narragansett Indians.

England under instructions to talk to Sir Ferdinando Gorges and the Council for New England, and to ask them to help get the Pilgrims out of the clutches of the Merchant Adventurers. When the *Charity* sailed, the pinnace *Little James* was tied behind her; the smaller ship was loaded with codfish and a supply of beaver worth 277 pounds. In the English Channel, pirates from the Barbary coast swooped down on the two ships. The *Charity* cut the *Little James* adrift, and the pinnace fell prize to the robbers.

In London, Standish had no luck in getting the help of Sir Ferdinando Gorges. But when he returned to Plymouth he brought three pieces of news with him: King James was dead, and his son, Charles I, was king; Deacon Robert Cushman had died of the plague in London; and their beloved former pastor at the Green Gate, John Robinson, had died in Leyden.

Since Standish's mission to London had failed, the Pilgrims set about immediately to think of how they might further expand the beaver trade and more quickly pay off their debts. Winslow sailed to Maine and opened trade with the Abnaki Indians on the Kennebec River, at present-day Augusta.

That year, not far from where Weston's men had built Wessagusset, a rival fur-trading post was set up which again threatened Plymouth's beaver trade on Boston Bay. Its founders—Captain Wollaston and Thomas Morton—were backed by Sir Ferdinando Gorges. Not far to the north of what

This nineteenth-century print shows Miles Standish and his men attacking Wituwamat and the Massachusetts Indian leaders during his raid on Wessagusset in March, 1623.

is now Quincy, Massachusetts, they established a trading post and colony, aided by a number of indentured servants, or bondsmen (men who had signed contracts to pay their passage money by working for their master for a certain number of years). They named the place Mount Wollaston.

The Pilgrims were angry to see a colony planted on land which they claimed as their own, but they made no move against it for the time being.

At the same time that Winslow was moving north into Maine, Plymouth also pushed south to Buzzards Bay, establishing a post at Aptucxet (Bourne) for trade with the Wampanoag and Narragansett.

The Dutch at New Amsterdam may have been alarmed to see the English

traders moving in their direction; for the Dutch eventually claimed all of Long Island and that part of Connecticut which lies west of the Connecticut River (as shown on the map which appears on pages 106-107).

If they were disturbed, the Dutch did not show their concern. New Netherland's Governor Peter Minuit wrote Bradford a friendly letter, offering to help him in any way he could. The Dutch afterward sent their chief trader at Fort Amsterdam, Isaac de Rasières, to Aptucxet and to Plymouth, where he offered the Pilgrims some information and some wampum. He explained to Bradford and others how valuable the ropes and belts of purple and white shell beads could be when used in trading with the Indians for beaver. Bradford said that, in time, it was wampum which "turned most to their profite."

In 1627—the year of Rasières' visit— Elder Brewster's wife, Mary, died. That year also saw the arrival in Plymouth of Governor Bradford's twelve-year-old son, John, who had been thought too young to make the trip on the *Mayflower* seven years before.

The following spring the Pilgrims turned their attention to Mount Wollaston. By this time Thomas Morton had quarreled with Captain Wollaston, and Morton had become sole head of the trading post. He renamed it Ma-re Mount (or "Mountain by the Sea") but the Pilgrims called it "Merie Mount." Bradford spoke of Morton as a "lord of misrule," and claimed to be shocked when he learned that the people at Merry Mount were "quaffing and drinking both wine and strong waters in great exsess." Bradford added: "They also set up a May-pole, drinking and dancing about it many days togeather, inviting the Indean women ... dancing and frisking togither."

Plymouth actually disliked Morton for a very different reason. He was trading guns and liquor to the Indians, who soon began taking their beaver pelts to Merry Mount rather than to Plymouth.

Morton admitted selling guns, but denied ever having supplied the Indians with drink. The angry Pilgrims warned him to stop the trade in firearms. When Morton refused, Plymouth sent a troop of men to Merry Mount under stubby Miles Standish (whom Morton later tauntingly referred to as "Captaine Shrimpe"). Standish had the Maypole cut down. After a brief skirmish, Morton was captured, brought to Plymouth, and sent back to Sir Ferdinando Gorges, in England, the following year.

Now the beaver trade began to thrive. In 1632, Edward Winslow was sent to the Connecticut Valley to found a trading post at Matianuck (Windsor) just north of present-day Hartford (where the enterprising Dutch were to build Fort Good Hope one year later, in 1633). That same year, after the Pilgrims had quickly set up a fort at Windsor, the Dutch sent a troop of seventy men from New Amsterdam against them, to warn the Pilgrims to leave their territory. When the Pilgrims refused, the Dutch withdrew rather than cause bloodshed. Elder Brewster's son Jonathan was in charge of the Matianuck post on the Connecticut in 1635 and 1636.

By means of Matianuck, Aptucxet, and posts like the one on the Kennebec, Plymouth continued to try to repay her debt to the Merchant Adventurers. There were to be many disappointments, however, before 1648, when Plymouth Colony finally shook herself completely free of debt.

In 1630, for example, the Pilgrim leader Isaac Allerton (who had married Fear Brewster) was discovered to have defrauded the colony of several thousand pounds—having debited the colony's funds for certain amounts he lost in trading ventures of his own. And in 1635, after a French force from Canada captured the Pilgrims' fur-trading post at Pentagoet (Castine), the Pilgrims were afraid that their other post on the Kennebec was in danger.

Plymouth then sent Edward Winslow to England with a petition to Sir Ferdinando Gorges, asking him to allow the colony to defend itself—by force, if necessary—against the Dutch in the Connecticut Valley and the

Though Plymouth's settlers called themselves Old Comers or First Comers, Americans knew them as "Pilgrims" by the 1840's. The term was taken from "they knew they were pilgrimes," a phrase found two lines from the bottom of the page in Bradford's Of Plymouth Plantation, *pictured at right.*

schisme amongst. 2. at ye first;

you wrote to mr martin, to preuente ye making of ye prouisions
ne kente, which he did, and sett downe his resolution, how much he would haue
of euery thing, without respecte to any counsell, or exception. surely he yt is in a
societie & yet regards not counsell, may better be a king, then consorte. To bs
shorte, if ther be not some other disposition setled unto then yet is; we yt should
be partners of humilitie, and peace, shall be examples of yangling, & insult-
ing. yet your money which you ther must haue, we will get prouided for you yt instant-
ly. 500li. you say will serue; for ye rest which hear, & in holand is to be used we may goe
scralch for it. for mr Crabe of whom you writs, he hate promised to goe with
us. yet as I tell you, yt shall not be without fears till I see him shipped, for he is much of-
posed. yet hope he will not faile. thinke ye best of all, and bear with patience what
is wanting, and ye lord guid us all.

your louing freind
Robart Cushman

London : June : 10.
An 1620.

I haue been ye larger in these things; and so shall craue leaue in some like passages
following, (though in other things ye I labour to be more contracte) that their children
may see with what dificulties their fathers wrasled in going through these
things in their first beginnings; and how god brought them along notwithstanding all their weaknesses, & infirmities. As also that some use may be made hereof in after times by others; yn shuch like waightie imployments, and herewith
I will end this chapter.

The .7. Chap.

Of their departure from Leyden, and other things
ther abute; with their ariuall at southhamton
wher they all mete togeather, and tooke in ther
prouisions.

At length after much trauell, and these debats; all things were got ready, and prouided. a small ship was bought, & fitted in holand, which was intended as to serue
to help them, so to stay in ye cuntrie, and atend upon fishing and shuch other afors
as might be for ye good, & benefite of ye colonie when they came ther. Another was
hired at London, of burden about 9 score, and all other things gott in readines. So
being ready to departe, they had a day of solemn humiliation, their pastor taking his
texte from Ezra. 8.21. And ther at ye riuer, by ahaua, yt proclamed a fast, that we might humble our selues before our god, and seeke of him a right way for us, and for our children, and for all our substance. upon which he spente a good parte of ye day very
profitably, and suitable to their presente occasion, the rest of the time was spente
In powering out prairs to ye lord, with great feruencie; mixed with abundance
of tears. And ye time being come that they must departe, they were acompani-
ed with most of their brethren out of ye citie, unto a towne sundrie miles of
called Delfes-Hauen wher the ship lay ready to receiue them. So they lefte ye
goodly & pleasante citie, which had been ther resting place nere 12 years; but
they knew they were pilgrimes & looked not much on those things; but lift up their
eyes to ye heauens their dearest cuntrie, and quieted their spirits. When they
come

French in Maine. But by this time King Charles had made the Archbishop of Canterbury, William Laud, head of a powerful new committee called the Commission for Regulating Plantations. Laud was Gorges' friend. But since he was a fierce enemy of Puritans and Separatists, the Pilgrims were afraid that he might close their meetinghouses and revoke their charter.

When Winslow brought his petition to Laud and Gorges, Laud would not discuss it. He preferred to scold Winslow for his Separatist beliefs. A quarrel developed, and Laud sent Winslow to jail for four months. Winslow returned to Plymouth soon after his release.

By this time Sir Ferdinando Gorges regretted that he had ever granted a charter to a group of Separatists as stubborn and troublesome as the Pilgrims. He and his friend the Archbishop now laid plans to send a troop of soldiers and some Church of England clergymen to New England. They intended to occupy the English settlements and to close their meetinghouses.

There were quite a number of permanent towns in New England, for by now several Puritan groups had founded Salem, Boston, and other towns just north of Plymouth, on Massachusetts Bay.

But before Gorges and Laud could send their troops to New England, troubles arose in England—troubles between King Charles and the Puritans—which would lead to revolution.

Late in the seventeenth century, both Plymouth's Pilgrims and the Puritans of Massachusetts Bay began building houses that are still treasured in New England, such as those shown here. They were larger and more comfortable than any of those of the early Pilgrims. The Parson Capen House, built in 1683 at Topsfield, Massachusetts, is seen at left; the beautiful Claflin-Richards House, right, arose in Wenham, in 1664.

Cavaliers and

The ascendancy of Charles I, just five years after the Pilgrims had founded Plymouth Colony, brought on a period of discontent in England—an era which culminated in a civil war. The war was climaxed, early in 1649, by the beheading of the King; and by the abolition of the House of Lords.

The unrest in England (1625-42) prior to the war caused a great wave of immigration to America and the West Indies, and brought to New England settlers far different from the Pilgrims.

These were the Puritans, who were as deeply religious as the Pilgrims, but

The long-haired dandy above is a Cavalier —a supporter of King Charles I. The man shown on the opposite page is Matthew Hopkins, an English witch-finder, whose book, Discoverie of Witches, *appeared in 1647.*

This cartoon of 1642 ridicules both of England's warring political groups: the Cavaliers of King Charles I, at left, and the Puritan "Roundheads," or supporters of Parliament, at right. The Puritans were called "Roundheads" because of their short haircuts. The two groups are shown here trying to get a dogfight started. The Cavaliers' dog may be Puddle, owned by King Charles's nephew, favorite, and strong ally, Prince Rupert.

Puritan Roundheads

hardheaded businessmen, where the Saints were far less shrewd.

In the Puritan ranks were successful merchants, well-to-do farmers, trades people—solid middle-class gentry.

A Puritan leader, John Endecott, described as an able, self-righteous, and fanatical man, on March 19, 1628, bought with six other "religious" persons a patent for territory in the Massachusetts Bay area from Gorges and the Council for New England.

Despite some opposition from Sir Ferdinando, a royal charter was granted the group on March 4, 1629. The

The four ships that Governor John Winthrop sent to New England are seen above in Boston harbor. They had arrived at Naumkeag (Salem) in early June, 1630; not finding enough open land, they sailed to Boston. Winthrop and three of his sons were aboard the Arbella, *at center.*

territory lay between the Charles and Merrimack rivers.

However, Endecott and his associates did not wait for the King's charter but proceeded with their plans for a settlement. On June 20, 1628, Endecott sailed from England on the *Abigail* with a small company. In September, he landed at Naumkeag and took over the small fishing post that had been established there two years before by exiles from Plymouth under Roger Conant. Endecott and his men soon drove Conant out of Naumkeag and claimed the land as their own. Conant and his men crossed the North River to found Beverly. Naumkeag was renamed Salem (from the Hebrew word

shalom, meaning peace) to celebrate the peace that followed.

After Endecott's people left for America, growing numbers of English Puritans considered migrating to New England. John Winthrop, a leading Puritan, was stripped of his position as an attorney in the Court of Wards because of his religious views.

As a result, Winthrop looked to New England, and with other Puritans set up the Massachusetts Bay Company. With Winthrop as governor, the Puritans then proceeded to organize a migration to the Massachusetts Bay area.

On March 29, 1630, four ships, the *Arbella,* the *Talbot,* the *Ambrose,* and the *Jewel* set sail from Yarmouth, Eng-

Sir Richard Saltonstall

Cotton

John Endecott

Sir Richard Saltonstall, a Puritan nobleman, joined the Massachusetts Bay Company in 1629 and sailed to America with Winthrop in 1630. John Cotton, who was a "forward" minister in England, was an old friend of Winthrop's; he came to Massachusetts in 1633, when his Puritanism was attacked by the Church of England.

John Winthrop

land, for America. These four vessels were the forerunners of some thirteen ships which carried more than one thousand Puritans to the Massachusetts Bay region during 1630 alone—about three times as many settlers as had come to Plymouth in the previous ten years.

Winthrop's fleet anchored at Salem. Not finding the situation of the colony to their liking, they went on to Boston harbor. There Winthrop founded a settlement at Charlestown, but finding the water supply bad, he soon moved on to Boston.

The Puritan settlers were energetic and resourceful. Within a very short time there were a number of towns in the Massachusetts Bay colony, including Dorchester, Medford, Watertown, Roxbury, and Lynn. The Pilgrims of Plymouth, who had been virtually the only settlers in New England for nearly a decade, now had more neighbors than they could cope with.

The Pilgrims, however, converted the Puritans to Separatism. In 1630, Deacon Samuel Fuller of Plymouth was sent to Boston, where he convinced Winthrop that the Puritans in America should break with the Church of England and adopt Plymouth's method of electing ministers for their churches. Winthrop agreed; and so, by way of the Puritans, the Pilgrims' traditions of democratic elections would continue long after Plymouth Colony had been swallowed up by its neighbors. In 1648 the Cambridge Synod, an assembly of New England ministers, met and adopted the Cambridge Platform. This Platform made the old Separatist tradition of Plymouth in matters of church government the accepted rule for all New England and formed the basis for the Congregational Church in which each congregation chose its own minister.

The Puritans, who prospered under Winthrop's governorship, had come to the New World well supplied with tools, goods, weapons, and equipment. Soon they would outstrip their Pilgrim neighbors. They were much richer than the Pilgrims and had made certain that their enterprises would succeed by preparing them in a businesslike manner. Gradually, Plymouth

Colony began to lose out economically to the Puritans of Massachusetts Bay. Massachusetts gained strength and power at the expense of Plymouth. The Puritans nibbled away at Plymouth's trading posts in Maine and in the Connecticut Valley and took over the valuable beaver trade.

Despite the disagreements that arose between Pilgrims and Puritans, both greeted England's Puritan Revolution of 1642 with full approval.

In England the Royalists (or Cavaliers), led by the nobility, had rallied to the side of King Charles I, who believed he should be supreme over Parliament. The tradesmen, artisans, and middle-class merchants took up the cause of the Presbyterian and Puritan Roundheads, who insisted Parliament had certain rights in the governing of England which the King could never take away. They insisted it must always be the right of Parliament—not the King—to levy taxes. After suffering severe military defeats at the hands of the Puritan Oliver Cromwell, who rose to leadership in the Civil War, the King's men were defeated in 1646.

The King was taken prisoner by the victorious Puritans. Fearing that the King's many supporters might try to restore him to supreme authority, the Puritan leaders decided to behead him in 1649. The country was to be ruled by Oliver Cromwell and by Parliament and was to be a Commonwealth rather than a monarchy.

Cromwell's victory was greeted enthusiastically in New England by both Puritans and Pilgrims alike. Edward Winslow, who had served three terms as Plymouth's governor, made another trip to London in 1646 on colonial business and, finding Oliver Cromwell in virtual control of the government, decided to remain. He spent the rest of his life serving England's Puritans. Winslow died in 1655 while acting as chief commissioner of an expedition

The drawings above left and below of English pikemen (foot soldiers whose chief weapon was a long, pointed spear or pike) appeared in a book published in 1637. They are demonstrating the various parade and battle positions a pikeman had to know in an age when battles were fought with much formality (see pages 126-127). Pikemen played a vital role in the battles of the English Civil War.

On June 14, 1645, King Charles's forces were defeated by the Parliamentary troops
Oliver Cromwell at Naseby, in Northamptonshire. This diagram shows royal forces
top and Parliamentary forces below. Cavalry form both wings of the battle lin

kemen (with spears raised) are in the middle, flanked by musketeers. Cromwell's
valry won the battle for him, and so gave him virtual military control of Eng-
nd. Because of their bravery, Cromwell and his cavalry were nicknamed "Ironsides."

John Milton (above), the great English Puritan poet, was to write, in 1649, a pamphlet defending Cromwell's execution of Charles I. Cromwell rewarded Milton by giving him a position in the Commonwealth government.

Cromwell sent to the West Indies to take Jamaica from the Spanish.

Governor William Bradford, in 1646, recalled his joy at hearing of Cromwell's victory when he wrote: "Full little did I thinke that the downfall of the Bishops, with their courts, cannons and ceremonies had been so neare . . . the tiranous bishops are ejected, their courts dissolved . . . their ceremonies useless and despised . . . Do you not now see the fruits of your labours, O all ye servants of the Lord? You have not only had a seed time, but many of you have seen the joyful harvest; should you not then rejoice? . . . and again say, Hallelujah!"

Bradford must have been particularly astounded to hear of what happened to the powerful Archbishop of Canterbury, William Laud, who was arrested in 1642. Laud, as primate of England, represented everything that had forced the Pilgrims to leave England. He believed that he had been chosen by God to be the religious leader of the people of England. He also believed that Charles I was King of England by Divine Right—by the will of God. Laud sincerely held that the Church of England was the only rightful Church in England. He took it to be his duty to destroy Separatists, Puritans, or anyone else who opposed the Church of England.

In order to accomplish what he felt was his religious mission, Laud had the full support of the King. Those who had opposed his religious laws had been prosecuted in the Archbishop's Court of the High Commission or in the King's courts. The dreaded Star Chamber—a secret council operated by the King and his advisors—had been Laud's favorite weapon against his enemies. The Star Chamber had sentenced men to be tortured, imprisoned, and put to death.

The higher the Puritan tide rose in England, the more rigid Laud had been in punishing Puritans.

Finally, in 1642, Laud was tried by the Puritan-dominated Long Parliament and accused of treason. Although the House of Lords found him inno-

King Charles I was beheaded outside White-hall Palace, London, on January 30, 1649. In this contemporary German engraving the King's headless body can be seen on the block (center), and the masked executioner is shown holding up the severed head (left).

cent, the House of Commons had found him guilty, and had had him executed in 1645.

The Puritan Revolution had a curious effect on the development of America. After the Puritans seized power in England, the steady flow of immigration to Massachusetts abruptly ended. There was now no need for noncomformists to leave home and endure the hazards of the New World: they were now rulers in England.

The defeated supporters of Charles I—the Royalists or Cavaliers—had every reason to want to leave England, and many of them came to Virginia.

Oliver Cromwell, who had adopted the title of Lord Protector of England in 1653 and became virtual dictator of the country, died in 1658.

Disillusioned with the harshness of Puritan rule, England turned once more to her ancient monarchy and, in 1660, placed Charles II, the son of

King Charles I

Oliver Cromwell

William Laud

The picture at right, painted by the American painter Benjamin West, shows Oliver Cromwell, in boots and cloak, dissolving the "Rump" of the Long Parliament in April, 1653. The Long Parliament had been holding sessions since November, 1640. The "Rump" sessions were those held after the December, 1648, purge of those members hostile to the growing control of Parliament by the army and Cromwell. It was the Long Parliament that made war on the King and condemned Archbishop Laud to death. The King was beheaded at the order of a Rump session. By 1653 Oliver Cromwell, now ruler of England, began to find Parliament's power troublesome. He dissolved it, prior to declaring himself Lord Protector and virtual dictator of England.

Charles I, on the throne from which his father had been driven.

The restoration of the monarchy did not mean, however, that the government of England was to become exactly as it had been in the days of James I and Charles I. In Cromwell's reign the importance of Parliament in governing the country had become so well established that the English people would never again let their monarch trample on the rights of Parliament. Also, the Courts of High Commission and the Star Chamber had been abolished and

were never restored. When Charles II came to the throne it was understood that Parliament was to have the right to levy taxes, and other powers; and it became possible for a man or a party to oppose a policy of the King and to remain safely within the government. The growth of the two-party system, which England and America have today, was made possible by the Puritan Revolution.

In the reign of Charles II, despite the presence in London of a government that was no longer sympathetic, Plymouth and Puritan Massachusetts continued to hold their radical religious views.

Seldom had there been men of such iron will and resolution. The Puritans flayed and persecuted religious nonconformists. Many non-Puritans lived in Massachusetts, having come there because of the generous terms of securing ownership of land. They had one choice—to conform or to get out. Most conformed.

There is no question that the Puritan code allowed its followers to be-

The cartoon above, which appeared in England in 1641, makes fun of lo[...] feltmakers and leather sellers who had decided to become "forward" mi[...] ters. The cartoon below, which appeared in 1653, shows Father Christ[...] (center) driven away by Puritans who no longer welcome him in Engla[...]

The dresses of these Englishwomen of 1640 (left and opposite) are pla[...] than those they would have worn before the Puritans began to gain po[...]

come excessively intolerant. The most outstanding examples of this fault were the witchcraft trials of 1692 in Salem and in other regions of Massachusetts. Some nineteen so-called witches were hanged or crushed to death at Salem.

Witch-hunting had spread like a contagious disease from Europe where it had become increasingly more common since the mid-fifteenth century.

The practice of witchcraft itself had long been considered a crime in England and in most of the rest of Europe. James I, who was a most superstitious man, wrote a book called *Daemonologie*, which dealt with the subject and advocated the death penalty for witches. In 1604 such a law was passed in England and was in effect when the Puritans first came to Massachusetts.

A witch was defined as one who was allied with the Devil and therefore evil. In those dark times, many persons afflicted with illnesses such as epilepsy were denounced as witches—for the seizures they suffered were considered signs that the Devil had possessed the individual, who then had to be destroyed. During the 1640's, a man named Matthew Hopkins declared that he had secret ways of uncovering witches and was appointed Witch Finder General. He went from place to place in England exposing "witches." The innocent persons—men, women, and children—executed on his testimony are estimated to have been numbered in the hundreds.

In Massachusetts, Cotton Mather was a leading witch-hunter and often

When "witch fever" struck New England, Judge Samuel Sewall (above left) was to become a leading judge in the witch trials that were held at Salem. It is quite likely that Sewall accepted evidence given by Cotton Mather (above right), a Puritan minister and scholar who thought himself to be well informed about witches and often testified against them.

testified as an expert at witch trials.

The Pilgrims never became involved in the tormenting of witches the way the Puritans did. At the height of the persecution only one person was charged with witchcraft by the Pilgrims in the town of Scituate. Mary Ingham was tried and acquitted of the charge of causing one Mehitable Woodworth "to fall into violent fitts . . . causing great paine unto severall parts of her body att severall times, soe as shee, the said Mehitable Woodworth, hath been almost bereaved of her sencis . . ."

But the witch fever soon burned itself out. The hysteria came to an end in the Old South Meeting House in Boston when Judge Samuel Sewall read out his confession of shame for the part he had played in the trails.

Sewall's action was only a small step forward, out of the dark, superstitious century in which he lived. Yet what had happened in the little town of Salem was happening in many different countries—and witches would continue to be hunted in Europe for many years to come.

In every age, man must try to take the forward step that Sewall took, because the dark power of superstition has to be conquered, over and over again, by every generation.

The nineteenth-century paintings below and at right capture all of the horror of the Salem witch fever. The girl below has just been accused of witchcraft. The girl at right has been convicted of the crime and is being led away to the tree where she will be hanged.

The Indian chief called King Philip was slain in 1676, in Rhode Island.

King Philip

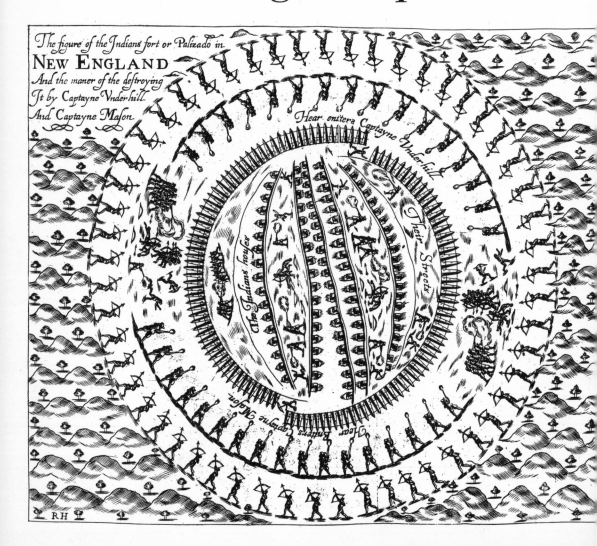

The figure of the Indians fort or Palizado in
NEW ENGLAND
And the maner of the destroying
It by Captayne Vnderhill
And Captayne Mason

Hear entera Captayne Vnderhill

The Indians howses

Their Streets

Hear Enters Captayne Mason

RH

In 1637, an ugly episode took place between whites and Indians. The Pequot, under a chief named Sassacus, were becoming increasingly irritated by the inroads being made into their lands. Pilgrims and Puritans had set up numerous trading posts in Connecticut, especially in the Connecticut River valley.

Clashes followed between Indians and traders in many areas. When the Indians killed a colonist, the colonists responded by killing Indians. Because of growing irritation on both sides, war broke out between Puritans and the Pequot.

It was a short conflict which ended in three weeks after a combined force of Massachusetts and Connecticut men, commanded by Captain John Mason and John Underhill surprised about 700 Pequot men, women, and children at an encampment near the mouth of the Mystic River in Connecticut.

The English fell on the Indians with musket, sword, and fire. Few Pequot escaped. Those of them who did were sold into slavery.

The slaughter of the Pequot was ghastly. Governor William Bradford described the overwhelming victory in these words: ". . . it was delightful to see them frying in ye fyre, and ye streams of blood quenching ye same."

The Pilgrims and Puritans almost universally regarded the New England Indians as "the dregs of mankind." The leader in the work of educating and converting them to Christianity was the Reverend John Eliot, a pastor from Roxbury who was gravely disturbed because the Indians were "so stupid and senseless."

He decided to learn their language and translate both the Lord's Prayer and the Ten Commandments, and even completed the ambitious project of translating the Bible into the Algonquian tongue. Eliot did convert a number of tribesmen in the 1640's, who were afterwards known as the "Praying Indians."

The Pequot War was a mere skirmish when compared to the great conflict that broke out in 1675 between the tribes of the Wampanoag Federation and the English. The struggle, known as King Philip's War, lasted a year and resulted in the downfall of the Algonquian tribes in New England.

King Philip, whose Indian name was Metacom, succeeded to leadership of the Wampanoag after the death of his elder brother, Wamsutta. Wamsutta had taken over command when his father, the respected Chief Massasoit died in 1661. After Wamsutta died at

The 1640 engraving at left shows the 1637 attack of Puritan soldiers and their Mohegan Indian allies on the Pequot fort at Stonington, Connecticut, where more than 600 Pequot died. The scene at right, taken from a 1676 map, shows Pilgrim soldiers fighting Indians.

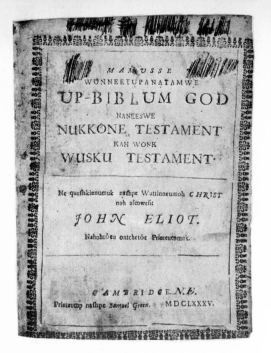

The 1659 portrait below pictures the Reverend John Eliot, the Puritan missionary known as the "Apostle to the Indians." The title page of the Bible he translated into the Indians' Algonquian tongue is shown above.

Plymouth, Philip became the king.

Missionary efforts to convert his people to Christianity particularly angered Philip, for he regarded the Christian doctrine of submission as an English trick to enslave his subjects.

In 1673, Edward Winslow's forty-four-year-old son, Josiah, "a worthie and well-accomplished gentleman" of Plymouth, became the first native-born colonial governor in America and the leader of the war against King Philip.

King Philip prepared for war with a skillfully executed diplomatic coup. He organized all the New England Indians to fight to regain their lands.

When a Praying Indian named Sassamon was murdered, Plymouth authorities blamed three of Philip's men for the deed and had two of them hanged and the third shot dead.

The Wampanoag Federation—which included the Abnaki, the Massachusetts, and the Mohegan—responded to this with war preparations. Reports came to Plymouth from outlying towns that Philip's men "were giving frequent alarums by drums and guns in the night . . . and the young Indians were earnest for war."

Although longtime friends of the Indians like Roger Williams and Samuel Gorton tried to avert bloodshed, all their overtures failed. The explosion awaited only the spark to set it off. It came on a day in June, 1675, when a settler at Swansea, Massachusetts,

The Wampanoag chief, King Philip, is seen at right in this nineteenth-century portrait.

shot and wounded an Indian trespassing on his land. It marked the start of New England's costliest Indian war.

Plymouth immediately set aside a day of fasting to entreat the Lord "to go forth with our forces, and blesse, succeed and prosper them."

Philip struck hard. He raided Dartmouth, Taunton, Middleborough, and other towns. Sweeping to the outskirts of Plymouth itself, he burned Scituate.

War erupted everywhere in New England. Tribe after tribe rallied to King Philip, and panic rose among the whites to such an extent that even the faithful Praying Indians, who lived in isolation on remote Cape Cod, were subjected to severe repressive measures by the Pilgrims. In spite of this treatment, the Praying Indians of Cape Cod gave faithful service to Plymouth as scouts and in combat.

As might be expected, the Massachusetts Puritans dealt with the Praying Indians even more harshly than had their Plymouth neighbors. When a group of two hundred recent converts to Christianity deserted and joined Philip, the Puritan Fathers drove the rest of the Praying Indians from their villages, set fire to their fields, and executed some of them on mere suspicion.

The alliance Philip had forged with the New England tribes proved to have a weak link. The Narragansett were longtime enemies of the Wampanoag. They could have been Philip's most potent allies, but refused to act in behalf of their ancient foes. And while

Both Pilgrims and Puritans persecuted Quakers. The unfortunate Quaker shown above was tied to a cart and whipped out of town.

they sulked in surly reluctance, a combined force of Connecticut, Plymouth, and Massachusetts men with a band of Mohegan allies made a forced march against the Narragansett stronghold on a fortified island in the Great Swamp near Kingston, Rhode Island.

At dawn on a bitter cold Sunday morning, late in 1675, the white men took the slumbering camp by surprise and butchered hundreds of men, women, and children. This blow smashed the Narragansett and proved fatal to Philip's cause; for with the Narragansett, Philip could have triumphed from Penobscot to Long Island Sound, and New England might have been wrested from the white men.

Many towns were left in ashes as

Philip's warriors struck Lancaster, Medfield, Mendon, Weymouth, Marlborough, Springfield, and Sudbury.

But by the spring of 1676, Philip's people were hounded on all sides. They had to keep on the move, living in forests and swamps.

Philip fought on, gradually working his way back to his home grounds on Mount Hope Neck near Sowams, Rhode Island, in the summer of 1676.

A Pilgrim detachment led by Captain Benjamin Church, a skilled Indian fighter, closed in on Philip. Church captured Philip's wife and son, killed some members of his family, and then moved against Philip, who had fled into the woods. A white man, Caleb Cook, and a Praying Indian, Alderman, set an ambush for Philip. Cook's gun misfired, but Alderman sent a ball into Philip's heart, and "he fell on his face in the mud and water . . ."

Church had Philip's head and hands cut off and left the body for the wolves. The hands were sent to Boston, and the head, carried in triumph to Plymouth, was placed on a pike on a watchtower where it bleached for twenty years, a nesting place for wrens.

With Philip's death the war was ended. The Indians were no longer a factor of any political importance in New England. But the white men did not win an easy victory. One man in sixteen of military age had been killed in the war against King Philip.

The ruthless treatment accorded King Philip was in keeping with traditional Puritan and Pilgrim behavior toward those who opposed them.

Among the first of many to feel the weight of Pilgrim disapproval had been Roger Williams, a young preacher who came to Plymouth in 1631 or 1632.

Williams had declared that "King James has no more right to give away or sell Massasoit's lands and cut and carve his country, than Massasoit has to sell King James' kingdom."

In addition to this, Williams crusaded against religious intolerance. He spoke out boldly for freedom of worship and gained some support in Plymouth. In 1634, Williams left that colony and went to Salem, where the congregation chose him as their pastor. But the Massachusetts Bay authorities wanted no such radical in their midst. Late in 1635, the court ordered his banishment from Massachusetts.

The modern painting below shows Roger Williams making his terrible journey from Massachusetts to Rhode Island early in 1636.

The portraits at left of Josiah Winslow and his wife, Penelope, were painted in London in 1651, probably by Robert Walker. The son of Edward Winslow, Josiah founded the first public school in Plymouth in 1674, and commanded the United Colonies' soldiers in King Philip's War.

Penelope Winslow   Josiah Winslow

Williams managed to get a stay until spring. But when he continued to preach, the authorities were so angered that they plotted to seize him and put him on a ship for England.

Friends warned Williams, and he fled into the wilderness—an exile—and was "sorely tossed for fourteen weeks in a bitter winter season not knowing what bread or bed did mean . . ."

He finally reached the country of the Wampanoag and settled at Seekonk, Rhode Island, near Sowams. Informed that he was still within the borders of Plymouth Colony, Williams moved on again, this time across Narragansett Bay where, with five supporters, he founded Providence, Rhode Island, which he hoped would always be "a shelter for persons distressed for conscience . . ." All who came there were granted full religious freedom.

By 1656, there was an influx of Quakers into New England, and the Pilgrims had to deal for the first time with the Society of Friends—as the Quakers called themselves.

The Quakers rejected baptism and communion, and recognized neither rank nor outside authority.

For these and other reasons, the Pilgrims, and the Puritans as well, denounced the Quakers as "madmen, lunaticks and daemoniacks."

The Quakers fought back. Once, at the meetinghouse in Cambridge, a Quaker burst in with a bottle in each hand. He shattered them and cried to the startled congregation, "Thus, will the Lord break you into pieces."

In 1643 the New England colonists· had met in Boston to decide an important issue: who was to protect them from invasion by France or Holland, for instance, while the English were fighting their bitter Civil War at home? Massachusetts, Plymouth, Connecticut, and New Haven solved the problem by joining together under a mutual defense agreement and formed the United Colonies.

And it was the United Colonies that took joint action on the matter of the Quakers in 1657, when a meeting in Plymouth resolved to get rid of the "troublesome pests" by driving them into the wilderness. A year later, the United Colonies, led by John Endecott, decided upon more drastic measures against the Quakers. They and all other "heretics" were to be driven from each of the colonies "under pain of death."

But despite their hatred of the Quakers, the Pilgrims did not go to the extremes practiced by the Puritans in their war on the Friends. Quakers caught by Puritans had their ears sliced off, their cheeks branded with hot irons, or were beaten insensible, flayed with tarred ropes, stripped of all possessions—even blinded and hanged.

But in all fairness, it must be stated that even among the Puritans such attitudes met with opposition from the rank and file and forced the Bay Colony officials to soften their unbending ways. The Quakers won much sym-

Painted in Massachusetts by an unknown artist around 1670, the picture at left, The Mason Children, *shows how Pilgrim and Puritan children dressed during the late 1600's.*

A
MIRROUR
or
LOOKING=GLASSE
For Saints, and Sinners

Wherin
is recorded, as Gods great
goodness to the one, so his severe
judgments against the other

Wherunto is added
The wondrous workes of God
in Nature

And the curious, costly, and
Stupendious workes made
by Man

With
The cheifest curiosities of An-
tient, and Moderne times

Jerusalem

Nineve

The strong religious convictions which sent Pilgrims and Puritans to America, and which brought civil war to England, had a lasting effect on men and ideas—as may be seen in this title page of an early eighteenth-century work by an English clergyman.

pathy and many converts in Plymouth by their bravery of spirit, a quality much admired by the Pilgrims.

While the English colonists in the New World struggled to meet the political and social problems with which they were faced, the English themselves had new problems in government which they too must solve.

In 1689 England, displeased by Stuart rule, brought William of Orange and his wife Mary (the daughter of James II) to the throne as constitutional monarchs. William and Mary proved to be liberal politically, and the colonial governments in America began to ask for favors at Court. Massachusetts, which gradually had come to dominate the United Colonies, learned that New York had asked the Crown for Plymouth. Massachusetts immediately put in a bid for Plymouth, too, and in October, 1691, was granted a royal charter for the colony. Boston told the surprised Pilgrims that they had taken the action because Plymouth could not defend itself if New York tried to seize it by force. After more than seventy years, Plymouth Colony was no more.

Early in July, 1692, the Plymouth General Court held its last meeting. As its final act, the body set aside the last Wednesday of August "to be kept as a day of sollemne fasting and humiliation."

The Pilgrims and the Puritans left

eir belief that all must seek e word of God in the Bible used Pilgrims and Puritans teach all boys and girls to ad. For this purpose horn- ooks were made, usually con- ting of the alphabet and a ble text, mounted on a ard and covered with a eet of transparent animal rn. Such a hornbook is seen right, while another is own in use, above. Later on, ildren used the New Eng- nd Primer, printed in Boston 1690. The first page of this imer is seen at far right.

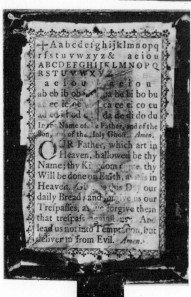

The most famous picture of the Pilgrims may be this painting by George H. Boughton, titled Pilgrims Going to Church. *It is inaccurate in that it does not show the Pilgrims climbing up Fort Hill, where their fort meetinghouse was actually located; but it is correct in showing them walking through the snow, carrying their guns and Bibles.*

Though spiritually strong, Plymouth was politically weak. She never dominated the United Colonies (as Massachusetts, Plymouth, Connecticut, and New Haven were known), and she was later absorbed by the Puritans of Massachusetts Bay. Yet Plymouth was victorious, for her Pilgrims have come to symbolize the faith and courage of millions.

an indelible mark on the rocky New England soil and on the people it produced through the centuries. While they were sometimes cruel and singularly narrow-minded, these flinty people also were conscientious, resolute, and determined—traits which were to play a vital part in shaping the destiny of the people who would one day be citizens of the United States.

The contributions of the Pilgrims and Puritans were many. They were the first to develop a church government in which elections were held yearly by the whole congregation. This democratic system was immediately put to use in the New England town meeting—and influenced the men who later formed the government of the United States. Connecticut championed civil liberties; Rhode Island, religious freedom. And public education for all was made compulsory in Massachusetts in 1647.

Both Puritans and Pilgrims considered it each man's duty to learn to read in order to be able to read the word of God in the Bible, and to perfect himself in all ways, in order to glorify God. Therefore, as early as 1624 the Pilgrims announced their intention of opening a common school, although the plan was delayed almost half a century by their lack of funds.

In 1636, Harvard College was founded at Cambridge. It was the first institution of higher learning in the English colonies and was to become one of the world's great universities.

Both Puritans and Pilgrims alike gave to America the idea that education is not the privilege of a few but the right of all.

By present-day standards, the Pilgrims of Plymouth Colony were almost as intolerant as the Puritans of Massachusetts Bay. But in the age in which they lived, tolerance was a new idea, believed by almost nobody, and to be found almost nowhere on earth.

And although the Plymouth settlers had journeyed as religious pilgrims to the New World in their search for freedom of conscience, true freedom of conscience for all men would not come until after the American Revolution.

But the Pilgrims possessed a strength that is still admired. Toward the end of his history, *Of Plymouth Plantation*, Bradford writes of the death, in April, 1643, of "My dear and loving friend, Mr. William Brewster."

"He was tender-hearted . . . of such as were in misery," wrote Bradford, and did the "best good he could . . . walking according to the light he saw, till the Lord revealed further unto him." He was a man, Bradford continued, who "had done and suffered much for the Lord Jesus . . . in this wilderness, and done . . . faithful service in his place and calling."

In speaking thus, Bradford spoke not only for Brewster, but for all that was best in the Pilgrim character. And it is because of the strength, the ideals, and the courage of men like William Bradford and William Brewster that the Pilgrims are so well remembered by Americans today.

The Pilgrims sometimes punished petty
offenders by putting them in the stocks.

AMERICAN HERITAGE PUBLISHING CO., INC.

BOOK DIVISION

Editor

Richard M. Ketchum

JUNIOR LIBRARY

Editor

Ferdinand N. Monjo

Assistant Editor

John Ratti

Editorial Assistants

Julia B. Potts • Mary Leverty

Malabar S. Brodeur • Judy Sheftel

Copy Editor

Naomi W. Wolf

Art Director

Emma Landau

Appendix

ACKNOWLEDGEMENTS: The editors are deeply grateful to Mr. George F. Willison for giving so generously of his knowledge of the Pilgrims; in addition they wish to thank the following individuals and organizations for their tireless assistance in furnishing pictorial information and material: Miss Rose T. Briggs, Director, and Mr. Harry H. Schnabel, Jr., of Pilgrim Hall, Plymouth, Massachusetts; Mr. E. Lawrence Couter, Director of Public Relations of Plimoth Plantation, Plymouth, Massachusetts; Mr. Timothy Green of London; Mr. John Mosly of Fuengirola, Spain; Mr. and Mrs. Ulrich Wever of Hannover, Germany; Mr. Samuel Chamberlain of Marblehead, Massachusetts; and Mrs. Jean R. Lange, Director of Public Relations of the Montclair Art Museum, Montclair, New Jersey.

PICTURE CREDITS

The source of each picture used in this book is listed below, by page. When two or more pictures appear on one page, they are separated by semicolons. The following abbreviations are used:

BM—British Museum
CS—Culver Service
JCB—John Carter Brown Library
M—Collection Mauritshuis, The Hague
MM—Metropolitan Museum of Art
MR—Musées Royaux des Beaux Arts

de Belgique
MSH—Massachusetts State House
NPG—National Portrait Gallery, London
NYHS—New York Historical Society
NYPL—New York Public Library

PH—Pilgrim Hall, Plymouth, Massachusetts
PP—Plimoth Plantation, Plymouth, Massachusetts
R—Rijksmuseum, Amsterdam
RT—Radio Times Hulton Picture Library

Maps and illustration of Plymouth drawn for this book by David Greenspan
Photographs of the Scrooby area in chapters II and III taken expressly for this book by John Bulmer

Cover: Detail from "Pilgrims Going to Church," —NYHS. **Front End Sheet:** MR. **Half Title:** S. A. Green, *Ten Facsimile Reproductions* — NYPL. **Title:** "Landing of the Pilgrims," anon. — Coll. Mrs. Robert B. Bowler, Plymouth. **Contents:** NYPL. 10 *Les Très Riches Heures du Duc de Berry*—Chantilly, Musée Condé; photo Giraudon. 11 Courtauld-Inst. of Art. 12 (left) Lucas Cranach — CS; (right) Emile Doumergue, *Iconographie calvinienne*—NYPL. 13 Wall painting in Chaldon Church, Surrey — Albert W. Kerr. 14 (all) NPG. 15 Anon.—Soc. of Antiquaries, London. 16 RT. 18-9 Nicolas J. Visscher — BM. 19 (bot.) Coll. Simon Wingfield Digby, M. P. 20 RT. 21 RT. 22-3 By courtesy of His Grace the Marquess of Salisbury. 25 NPG. 26 (both) RT. 29 (bot.) Coll. Sir Ronald Lechmore. 30 (both) H. D. Traill, *Social England*—NYPL. 31 Traill, *op. cit.*—NYPL. 33 PH. 38-9 "Scene on Ice," Hendrick Avercamp — M. 40 J. Allan Cash. 43 "Die Alte Borse zu Amsterdam," Job A. Berckheyde — Stadelsches Kunstinstitut, Frankfort. 45 "Die Wollwascherei," Pieter de Molijn—courtesy Walter Bernt, Munich. 46-7 "View of Haarlem," Jacob van Ruisdael—M. 49 "Le Repos du Tisserand," Adriaen van Ostade and Cornelius Decker —MR. 50-1 NYPL. 53 "A Quay at Leyden," Jan van der Heyden—MM. 54 (top) Gemeente-Archief Te Leiden; (bot.) R. 56-7 "Marriage Festival," David Teniers the Younger—MM. 58 (both) PH. 59 RT. 60 "L'Offre Galante," Jan Steen—MR. 62-3 "Dutch Seascape," Van de Velde—PH. 65 Dutch School—*Harper's Weekly*, March 9, 1895. 66-7 "Old London Bridge," Claude de Jongh—Victoria and Albert Museum. 68 David F. Lawlor from A. Devaney. 69 Duhamel du Monceau, *Traité Général des Pesche*—NYPL. 70 (top) NPG.

71 Lib. of Congress. 73 (top) Louis Lacroix, *Les Derniers Morutiers Français*—Pub. Arch. of Canada; (bot.) NYPL. 74-5 M. 76 NYPL. 78-9 (both) BM. 80 RT. 83 "Sailing of the Pilgrims from Plymouth, England," Charles Shimmin—Woolaroc Museum, Bartlesville, Okla.. 84 Plan of the *Mayflower* adapted by Cal Sachs. 86-7 Pix Inc. 89 "Signing of the Compact," Percy Moran—PH. 90-1 "*Mayflower* in Plymouth Harbor," William Halsall — PH. 93 Champlain, *Voyages* — JCB. 94-5 "Landing of the Pilgrims," Michael Corné—PH. 95 The Dickinsons, Plymouth. 96 PP. 97 "The Pilgrims Holding Their First Meeting for Public Worship in America," Georg Johann Schwartze—PH. 98 "Samoset Bids the Pilgrims Welcome at Plymouth," Charles Hoffbauer — New England Mutual Life Insurance Company. 99 (top) PH; (bot.) The Dickinsons. 100 "The First Thanksgiving," Doris Lee—John Hancock Mutual Life Insurance Company. 102 PH. 103 (all) PH. 104 PH. 107 Cartouche: *Beschrijuinghe Van Virginie, Nieuw Nederlandt, Nieuw Engelandt*—NYPL. 108 (top right) Justin Winsor, *Memorial Hist. of Boston*—NYPL; (rest) PH. 111 PP. 114 Malabar S. Brodeur. 115 NYPL. 117 MSH. 118 & 119 Samuel Chamberlain. 120 Traill, *op. cit.*—NYPL. 120-21 Traill, *op. cit.*—NYPL. 121 Matthew Hopkins, *Discoverie of Witches*—NYPL. 122-23 "Arrival of Winthrop's Ships in Boston Harbor," Halsall—Coll. Miss Madeleine Ellis. 123 (left) CS; (mid.) MSH; (top right) Anon.—Mrs. Richard M. Saltonstall; (bot. right) Amer. Antiquarian Soc. 124-25 Henry Hexham, *Principles of the Art Military*—Yale University Lib. 126-27 Coll. Mrs. John Nicholas Brown. 128 NYPL. 129 RT. 130 (top & mid.) NPG; (bot.) Sir Anthony van Dyck—Lambeth Palace, London. 131 "Oliver Cromwell

Dissolving the Long Parliament, April 1653," Montclair Art Museum. **132** (top) RT; (bot. left) Wenceslaus Hollar, *Ornatus Muliebris Anglicanus*—Pierpont Morgan Lib.; (bot. right) *History Today.* **133** (top left) Mass. Hist. Soc.; (top right) NYPL; (bot.) Hollar, *op. cit.*—Pierpont Morgan Lib. **134** "Accused of Witchcraft," Douglas Volk—Three Lions, courtesy Mrs. Robert Simons. **135** "The Witch Hill," Thomas S. Noble—NYHS. **136** (top) CS; (bot.) John Underhill, *News from America*—NYPL. **137** John Seller—JCB. **138** (top) NYPL; (bot.) Henry E. Huntington Lib. **139** Shelburne Museum. **140** Samuel Seyer, *Memoirs Historical & Topographical of Bristol*—NYPL. **141** Frederick Rothermel—Rhode Island Hist. Soc. **142** (both top) PH; (bot.) Coll. Mr. Nathaniel Hamlen. **144** Traill, *op. cit.*—NYPL. **145** (top) Andrew White Tuer, *History of the Hornbook*—NYPL; (bot. both) NYPL. **146-47** NYHS. **149** Benson J. Lossing, *Our Country*—NYPL. **151** Mrs. Roger A. Pryor, *The Mother of Washington*—NYPL. **Back End Sheet:** "Tribunal of the Inquisition,"—San Fernando Royal Academy of Fine Arts, Madrid.

BIBLIOGRAPHY

Adams, Charles Francis. *Three Episodes in Massachusetts History.* Boston: Houghton, Mifflin, 1892.

Adams, James Truslow. *Epic of America.* Boston: Little, Brown, 1931.

——. *The Founding of New England.* Boston: Atlantic Monthly Press, 1921.

Ames, Azel. *The Mayflower and Her Log.* Boston: Houghton, Mifflin, 1901.

Andrews, Charles M. *Colonial Period of American History,* Vol. I. New Haven: Yale University Press, 1934.

Arber, Edward. *The Story of the Pilgrim Fathers.* Boston: Houghton, Mifflin, 1897.

Bailey, Alfred G. *The Conflict of European and Eastern Algonkian Cultures from 1504 to 1700.* Sackville, New Brunswick: The Tribune Press, 1937.

Bartlett, W. H. *The Pilgrim Fathers.* London: A. Hall, Virtue, 1854.

Baxter, James Phinney. *Sir Ferdinando Gorges and his Province of Maine.* 3 vols. Boston: The Prince Society, 1890.

Beard, Charles A. and Mary R. *The Rise of American Civilization.* New York: Macmillan, 1930.

Beston, Henry. *The Book of Gallant Vagabonds.* New York: George H. Doran, 1925.

Bradford, William. *Of Plymouth Plantation.* Samuel Eliot Morison, ed. New York: Alfred A. Knopf, 1952.

Commager, Henry S., and Morison, Samuel E. *The Growth of the American Republic.* New York: Oxford University Press, 1950.

Cunningham, W. *The Growth of English Industry and Commerce,* Vol. II. Cambridge: Cambridge University Press, 1910.

Dexter, Henry Martyn, and Dexter,

Morton. *The England and Holland of the Pilgrims.* Boston: Houghton, Mifflin, 1905.

Durant, Will. *The Reformation.* New York: Simon and Schuster, 1957.

Flannery, Regina. *An Analysis of Coastal Algonkian Culture.* Washington, D.C.: Catholic University of America Press, 1939.

Force, Peter (ed.). *Tracts and Other Papers Relating Principally to the Origin, Settlement and Progress of the Colonies in North America.* 4 vols. Washington, D.C.: Peter Force, 1836-46.

Hart, Albert B. (ed.). *American History Told by Contemporaries,* Vol. I. New York: Macmillan, 1897.

Howe, Henry F. *Early Explorers of Plymouth Harbor, 1525-1619.* Plymouth: Plimoth Plantations, Inc., and the Pilgrim Society, 1953.

Innes, Arthur D. *A History of England and the British Empire.* 4 vols. New York: Macmillan, 1913.

Innis, Harold A. *The Cod Fisheries: The History of an International Economy.* New Haven: Yale University Press, 1940.

Jameson, J. Franklin (ed.). *Voyages of Samuel de Champlain, 1604-1618.* New York: Barnes & Noble, 1946.

Kinnecutt, Lincoln N. *The Settlement of Plymouth Contemplated Before 1620.* Washington, D.C.: United States Printing Office, 1920.

Lawson, John H. *The Hidden Heritage.* New York: Citadel Press, 1950.

Lorant, Stefan. *The New World.* New York: Duell, Sloan & Pierce, 1948.

Motley, John L. *The Life and Death of John of Barneveld.* London: J. Murray Publishers, 1874.

Mourt, G. (Pseudonym for Edward Winslow and William Bradford). *The Journal of the Pilgrims and*

Plymouth, in New England, in 1620. New York: J. Wiley, 1849.

Muzzey, David S. *The Heritage of the Pilgrims.* Washington, D.C.: United States Printing Office, 1920.

Parker, Arthur. *The Great Algonkian Flint Mines at Coxsackie.* Rochester, N. Y.: New York State Archaeological Society, 1925.

Parrington, Vernon L. *Main Currents in American Thought: The Colonial Mind,* Vol. I. New York: Harcourt, Brace, 1954.

Plumb, J. H. (ed.). *Studies in Social History—A Tribute to G. M. Trevelyan.* London: Longmans Green, 1955.

Prince, Thomas. *A Chronological History of New England.* Boston: Kneeland & Green, 1826.

Rowse, A. L. *The Elizabethans and America.* New York: Harper & Bros., 1959.

——. *The England of Elizabeth.* New York: Macmillan, 1951.

Smith, Abbott E. *Colonists in Bondage.* Chapel Hill, N. C.: University of North Carolina Press, 1947.

Smith, Bradford. *Bradford of Plymouth.* Philadelphia: Lippincott, 1951.

Smith, Captain John. *Description of New England.* London: Humfrey & Lownes, 1616.

Tawney, Roger H. *Religion and the Rise of Capitalism.* New York: Harcourt, Brace, 1926.

Trevelyan, G. M. *History of England.* Garden City: Doubleday, 1953.

Willison, George F. *The Pilgrims Reader.* Garden City: Doubleday, 1953.

——. *Saints and Strangers.* New York: Reynal and Hitchcock, 1945.

Wissler, Clark. *Indians of the United States.* Garden City: Doubleday, 1940.

FOR FURTHER READING

Young readers seeking further information on the Pilgrims and Plymouth Colony will find the following books to be both helpful and entertaining:

Anderson, Anita. *Squanto and the Pilgrims.* Chicago: Wheeler, 1949.

Carpenter, Francis. *Pocahontas and her World.* Alfred A. Knopf, 1957.

Criss, Mildred. *Mary Stuart.* New York: Dodd, Mead, 1939.

Daugherty, James. *The Landing of the Pilgrims.* New York: Random House, 1950.

Davis, William S. *Life in Elizabethan Days.* New York: Harper & Bros., 1930.

Firth, Charles. *Oliver Cromwell and the Rule of the Puritans in England.* New York: G. P. Putnam's Sons, 1900.

Hall-Quest, Olga. *How the Pilgrims Came to Plymouth.* New York: E. P. Dutton, 1946.

Jackson, Shirley. *The Witchcraft of Salem Village.* New York: Random House, 1956.

Longfellow, Henry W. *The Courtship of Miles Standish.* Boston: Houghton, Mifflin, 1920.

Matthews, Basil. *The Argonauts of Faith.* New York: George H. Doran, 1920.

Morison, Samuel Eliot. *The Story of the "Old Colony" of New Plymouth.* New York: Alfred A. Knopf, 1956.

Norman, Charles. *Flight and Adventures of Charles II.* New York: Random House, 1958.

Pine, Tillie. *The Pilgrims Knew.* New York: Whittlesey House, 1957.

Smith, Bradford. *William Bradford: Pilgrim Boy.* Indianapolis: Bobbs-Merrill, 1953.

Taylor, Duncan. *The Elizabethan Age.* New York: Roy Publishers, 1954.

Trachsel, Myrtle. *Elizabeth (Howland) of the Mayflower.* New York: Macmillan, 1950.

Tunis, Edwin. *Colonial Living.* New York: World Publishing, 1957.

Vance, Marguerite. *Elizabeth Tudor.* New York: E. P. Dutton, 1954.

Index

Bold face indicates pages on which illustrations appear

153